HARDPRESS.NET
HOME OF HARD-TO-FIND BOOKS

Livonian Tales
by Elizabeth Eastlake

Address:
HardPress
8345 NW 66TH ST #2561
MIAMI FL 33166-2626
USA
Email: info@hardpress.net

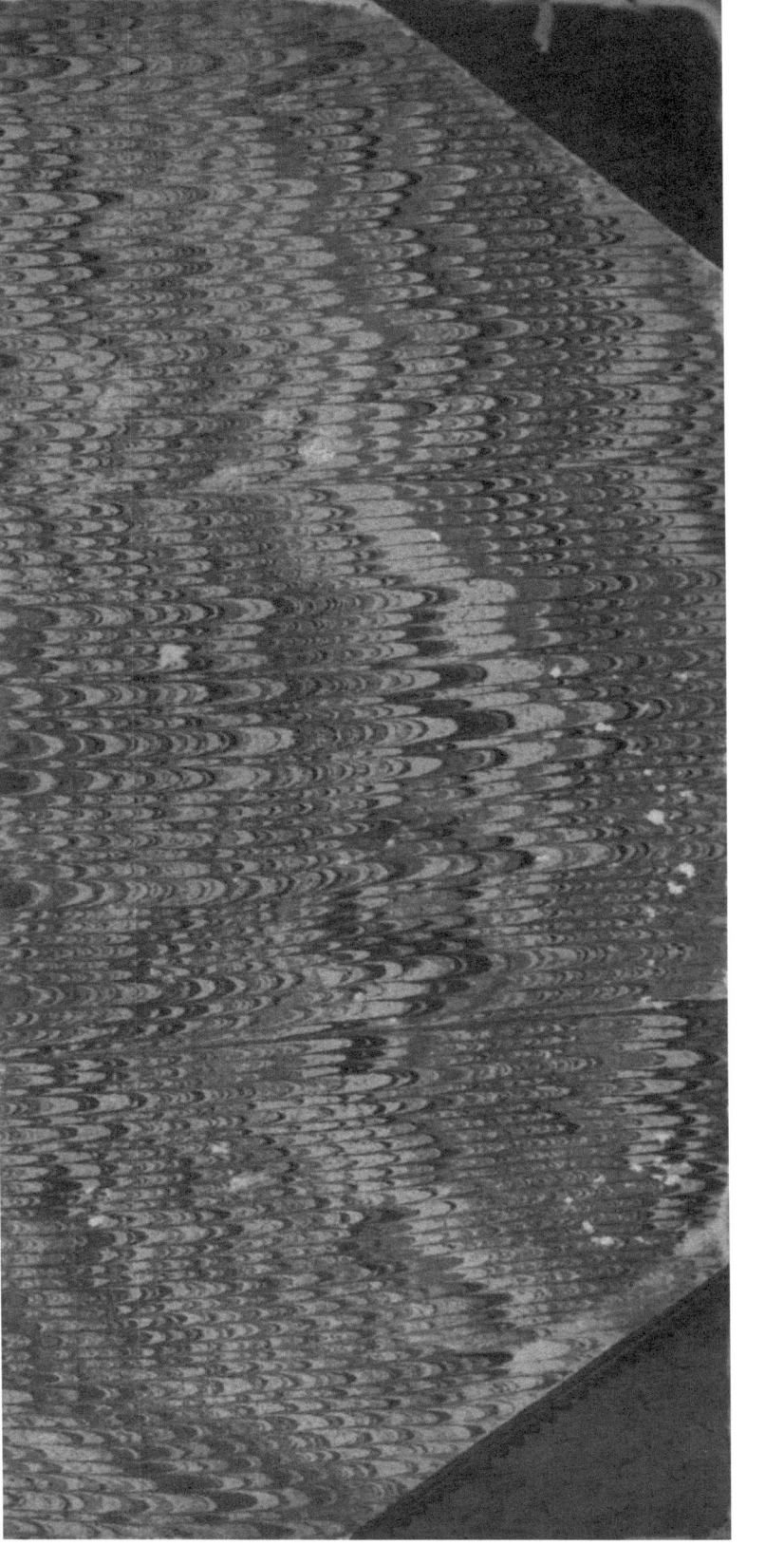

LIVONIAN TALES.

THE DISPONENT. THE WOLVES.
THE JEWESS.

BY THE

AUTHOR OF "LETTERS FROM THE BALTIC."

LONDON:

JOHN MURRAY, ALBEMARLE STREET.

1849.

10-3-78

CONTENTS.

LIVONIAN TALES.

THE DISPONENT.

CHAPTER I.

In the common style of colloquial intercourse to be met with in what is usually denominated general society—namely, that periodical collision of a number of persons, of which a large majority repeat what they hear, and a small minority think what they say, and those by no means all think rightly—it naturally follows that the emptiest sophistries will pass current equally as well as the profoundest truths—nay, generally much better; as, like all meretricious imitations, they are most calculated to please common eyes at first sight. A favourite futility which, as such, has doubtless never been out of vogue at any time, but which from the peculiar character of the age enters largely into the small-talk of respectable people of the present day, consists in extolling the simplicity which accompanies a state of nature, and lamenting the refinements which follow in the train of civilization. Implying by the first, that fabulous purity, when, "wild in woods the noble savage ran;" and by the second, those perverted luxuries to which a false cultivation has given birth; and thus contriving to give in one breath a wrong idea to a right definition, and a wrong definition to a right idea.

The simplicity of savage life! God help the poor creatures! Where is there the most perverted artificiality of the falsest and foulest civilization that can for one instant be compared with it? If there be a state of society where it seems to have become natural to man to outrage Nature; if there be a scene on which the angels of heaven must gaze with tears of pity—if so keen a pang as that of a helpless sympathy be permitted to mingle with their bliss;—it is when the brute force and the brute will of uncivilized man are left to riot without control—when not his nature, but its corruption, is the law of his life.

Even in those countries where the lowest orders of peasantry are nominally civilized, because nominally Christianized, but where want, oppression, and ignorance leave them but a degree better than the savage, the same facts support the same arguments. The simplest comforts, within every one's reach, are the last they care for—the natural affections within every heart, the last they indulge—their habits are senseless—their social relations artificial—their very costume frequently studiously inconvenient—the simple dictates of the law of Nature, in short, the last to which they resort. When people, therefore, talk of the simplicity of Nature and the refinements of civilization as anti thetical qualities, they are only idly repeating what has been but idle repetition ever since people have talked at all. In point of fact, these are synonymous things; that difference only existing which must ever exist between a divine idea and a human reality. If the much-to-be-desired simplicity of a state of nature be not among us, or rarely so, it is because we are too little refined and civilized, and not too much. For it is only in the paths of Christian wisdom, goodness, knowledge and sense, that such a state can be attained; and such real and only civilization is man's real and only nature.

Is it not a mystery, for instance, that in those parts of the world where man is nursed on poverty's hardest fare, and bred among Nature's roughest scenes, the choice of a wife, instead of being the voluntary act of the natural feelings of the heart, should be conducted upon a system only to be compared in manner with the regular *mariage de convenance* of the most artificial nation in the world, and in motives with the mercenary heartlessness of the vitiated worldling of any time or country? Yet this is the case in many countries that might be mentioned, the North American Indians included, and especially in the German provinces of Russia, wrested from Sweden during the last century, where the scene of our narrative lies;—marriages here being contracted through the intervention of a third person, and frequently without the parties having once met—or where previous acquaintance does exist, simply because that circumstance has afforded the gentleman the opportunity of judging of the lady's capacity for labour, or of ascertaining the amount of her dowry.

The usual form on these occasions is for the young man to engage the services of an old woman, who usually officiates for a whole parish in succession, to propose to the girl of whose qualifications he has heard the requisite report. The old woman sets about her business very cleverly—dwells on the good looks or fine disposition of her client, and especially on the vehemence of his attachment—for even a savage knows the sort of flattery most acceptable to a woman's heart. If she succeed in obtaining a favourable answer, the parties meet, frequently for the first time in their lives, the following Sunday at the clergyman's house, for the ceremony of betrothal; if not, the old woman is sent to a succession of ladies on a similar errand until she does —for when once a Livonian peasant has made up his mind to be married, he thinks the sooner he gets it over the better.

It was a fine morning in the month of March, the earth lay deep in her case of snow, but the sun was bright and early on its road, and, in spite of the winter landscape, there was a feeling of spring in the earliness of dawn ; that feeling, indeed, which is most trying to the southern-born foreigner, as reminding you of what other countries are already enjoying, and which here is still long to be " the hope deferred which maketh the heart sick." With the clergymen of these remote regions the Sunday is always, independent of its religious duties, a day of much occupation ; for the peasants, of which their congregations are solely composed, and who frequently come from great distances, take the opportunity, either before or after the services, for consulting their pastor on such matters wherein his advice or assistance can be of use, and these are not a few.

The worthy pastor of this district was already up and preparing for the duties of the day, when he was summoned into the little room set aside for the registerial business of his office—no sinecure beneath the jealous fancies of the Russian government— and where he always received his humble visitors. He was a good man, and very popular with his peasantry, who, if their

pastor be not their friend, rarely know any other; and to whose
spiritual, worldly, and bodily ailments he was in the habit of
administering as far as lay in his power;—to the first, as well as
any Christian dignitary in the world; and to the two latter, as
far as very slender means and homely knowledge permitted. On
this occasion, however, his help was required in another way;
for on entering the room he found a couple awaiting that ceremony of betrothal which in these remote districts is still the
relic of a faith of richer poetry amidst the poverty of Lu-
theranism.

The pastor was a theorist in the way of physiognomical expression, and had had so much opportunity for study in the raw
and rough countenances of his poor parishioners, that he fancied
he knew not only what a countenance said, but what it concealed
as well. In this latter respect they gave him perhaps the most
opportunity for observation, for many a poor peasant stood ab-
jectly before him with that stolid vacuity of expression in which
it required a nice eye to pronounce between the crust of habit
and the kernel of nature. In such occasions as this too he was
doubly interested to examine; for the ceremony of betrothal,
although not binding in law, has been made by long custom as
much so in feeling as that of marriage which follows it.

In the present instance there was much to occupy him in the
party, which consisted of three persons—a young girl, a middle-
aged man, and an old man—and the pastor looked with an
earnest and scrutinizing glance from the one to the other, as
the girl and the old man came forward in turn, kissed his hand,
and then made that painfully humble, yet not ungraceful inclina-
tion of the body, accompanied by a supplicatory action with the
hands, which is the national obeisance of this people.

There is much in the habits of obeisance and salutation among
the lower orders of a country, which tells you either the form
of religion or the mode of government—here it seemed no less
to deprecate tyranny and injustice than to testify respect. This
done, both the parties stood stock still, and the middle-aged
man, or the bridegroom, for such he was, having merely made a
servile bow, stepped up to the girl's side. She was pretty, and
very young; hard and vacant labour had not yet furrowed her
forehead, nor exposure to the air embrowned her skin; her hair

too, which, as with all the inhabitants of these regions, man and woman alike, was allowed to grow its full length, was bright-coloured and glossy, and fell in pretty waves upon her shoulders, and not too much over her face; while the little hollow circle of pasteboard, which the maidens of this part of the province wear fastened on the crown of the head, accorded gracefully with the round and flowing lines of her young face, and was easily ima-gined to represent a bridal chaplet for the occasion. The figure too, which was enclosed in the tight-fitting short-waisted spenser of coarse grey homespun cloth, was slight, easy, and round. The gay striped petticoat hung slimly down, and altogether, with the bent head and downcast eye, there could be no prettier picture of a Northern maiden on her betrothal day. So far, all was in character with the occasion; yet there was something also too foreign to it to be overlooked. The pastor was accustomed to all kinds of manner, from the most incomprehensible apathy to the most awkward sheepishness; but in that of the young girl there was something distinct from either. Her hands, which partook of the general delicacy of her whole appearance, were nervously restless; and, when she looked up for a moment, she showed an expression of bewilderment neither natural to her age nor to the occasion. Then she exchanged a few petulant whispers with the old man behind her, evidently her father, with far more hurry of manner than usually ruffles the dull surface of a Livonian woman's soul—in which expostulation seemed the cha-racter on one side, and pacification on the other. Behind them, on a chair, lay a gay piece of chintz, some red beads, and other articles of woman's finery, which the bridegroom brings on such occasions, and to which the old man pointed once or twice in furtherance apparently of his words. But this appeal was more violently resisted than any other; and she looked as if she would have spoken aloud, when, observing the minister's eye was upon her, down went the head again, and she stood immoveable.

The man, who stood firm at the girl's side, was anything but a match for her in appearance. He was a coarse ugly fellow, of above forty years of age, with reddish hair, watery eyes, and a large mouth. His face was bluff and full; but whether it was very open or very impudent, very honest or very much the re-verse, the pastor could not determine. He was evidently rather above the condition of a peasant; wore his hair short, and his clothes of the common coat and waistcoat cut. He was very much at his ease, and seemingly well pleased with his bride; from whom, however, he never got so much as a look.

The clergyman now addressed a few questions to each, as is usual on such occasions, relating to their knowledge of the fundamental doctrines of Christianity. The man answered with tolerable readiness and accuracy; but the young lady was not very audible in her replies, and her confusion increased so much, that, knowing she had passed through the rite of confirmation but a year before, the pastor thought it would be charity to shorten this part of the ceremony. He therefore proceeded at once to an exhortation upon the duties and obligations of married life—given with much feeling and good sense, but combined with particulars which, to a stranger, might have appeared ludicrous. He reminded the man that he did not take a wife only for the convenience of having his clothes mended, nor the woman a husband only for the privilege of wearing a matron's cap; that the wedding feasting would be soon over, and the wedding presents soon spent; that there would be much need for hard labour, and little time for idle pleasure; but that honest labour would be their pleasure, if there were love and harmony beneath their roof. That it was to be their high privilege to help one another in the burthens of this life, and their higher privilege still to encourage one another on the road to a better one. And besides this, and similar admonitions which they could understand, he added as much that they could not— knowing from experience that this would probably leave the deeper impression of the two.

He then asked the man, Ian, whether he was willing to be betrothed to this girl, Anno, and whether he was able to maintain her in comfort; to the first of which questions he received an immediate affirmative; and, to the other, the information that he was *Disponent* or Bailiff upon a neighbouring estate, which indeed he already knew, and which was in itself sufficient guarantee for the comforts of Anno's future establishment.

The pastor therefore turned to the girl with a much diminished sense of the disparity between her tender youth and the bridegroom's coarse maturity. It was true, the report of the peasants did not speak very favourably of the latter ; but in a country where the general character of the people is phlegmatic and inert, and the general standard of maintenance too often only a degree above starvation, he knew that the preferences of the heart could have little chance against the creature-comforts of a somewhat lower region. Nor, in spite of the words hardly cool from his lips, and a little warm stock of poetry close at his heart, could he altogether condemn this mode of reasoning. So he reached out his hand to one side of his table for a piece of paper, and began writing the short form of betrothal to which they were to put their names or marks. Then looking up for a moment with a kind expanding countenance,

" Well, Anno ! are you willing to have this man ?" and continuing to write,

" I am glad you are to have a comfortable home—mind you keep it clean and tidy—I 'll come and see you. I know you have been a good daughter, so I hope you 'll make a good wife : are you willing to marry Ian ?" No answer came ; and the old gentleman having finished writing his formula, looked up now in expectation. The poor girl's hands were pinched together, colourless and blue ; and her face was crimson, at least so much of it as could be seen, which was only the forehead and the division of the hair, from which a few slender strands hung straight down at right angles from the face. As the pastor looked up more inquiringly still—down went the head lower and lower—the whole hair fell over her as a veil, and the next moment face and hair and all were buried in her hands, and she burst out crying. The old father now came forward coaxingly, and whispered into her ear : she took no notice. The bridegroom took one of her hands to pull it from her face ; she elbowed him violently away, and seemed from her excited action as if she could gladly have struck him. " *Ei, Ei—Polli üchtige?*" " Nothing at all," said the old man ; " she is frightened."

" Women are silly," said the bridegroom—such forms of speech being quite consistent in Livonia with the most ardent passion—" give me the paper to sign."

" No, no," said the clergyman, " if you please, I 'll hear more about this first. Come with me, Anno ; there is nothing to be afraid of:" and he took the girl by the hand, who followed with choking sobs and heaving shoulders into the next room.

Here the mystery was soon solved; and through tears, and blushes, and hesitations, the pastor was made to understand that Ian might be a very good man, she dare say he was, but that he was not the man she had expected to be betrothed to—and this made all the difference to her—indeed—indeed it did—and she asseverated it with the utmost earnestness, as if fearing the pastor might not believe her. The old man smiled in his sleeve, but asked her in a serious tone why she had not said this at first, as it was committing a great fault to stand up and be betrothed to a man she did not wish for. Anno assented mutely, and the hair fell down again. Then with a slight degree of embarrassment, for the *affaires de cœur* of his poor parishioners were quite a new field to him, he gently questioned her how the mistake came about; and inquired finally as to the real Simon Pure of her affections. The answer was simple enough. She had seen a young peasant several times at church, whom she had taken, she knew not why, for the *Disponent* of Essmeggi, and when the old mother came with an offer of marriage from the actual *Disponent* himself, she had immediately agreed to his proposal of betrothal on the following Sunday. That she had never seen this Ian before; or rather, she had never looked at him; and when she did look at him this morning, she thought she should have died!

The pastor was both amused and touched at this narrative. He was accustomed to see the gentleness of the Lettish women crushed into apathy, or their quickness sharpened into cunning, and such an outbreak of genuine feeling was quite refreshing to him. He left Anno where she was, and returned alone into the little room. His blood was up to think that two men, one her father and the other old enough to be so, should combine to take advantage of a poor girl's mistake. Both were standing as he left them—the *Disponent* looking bold and undisconcerted, the old man cringing and shamefaced. He addressed this latter first, and not in gentle tones nor terms :—

" You old rascal !" he said, " to sell your little daughter for a few sacks of meal and tubs of *Strömlin*. Is that the way to heaven? and you about to leave this earth ! You should be ashamed of yourself: go home and work for her, and be glad this sin is off your grey head—it will be time enough for her to marry five years hence !"

The old man looked the type of ineffable sheepishness ; he whined out something about the *Disponent's* having come a long way on purpose—and the pastor being all ready; and about women having long hair, but short thoughts—a favourite proverb with the lords of the creation in this part of the world—and other silly excuses, which were suddenly silenced by an emphatic " Hold your tongue."

Then turning to the *Disponent,* the pastor said, " And you too—you great selfish fellow, to care to profit by what was never intended for you ! What blessing could you expect ? Go and get a wife honestly, if one will have you ; but don't come to me to help you to entrap a girl who likes somebody else better !"

As he said this he looked full at the man, and from that moment had no further doubt of his real expression. The slightest change had converted the countenance from one of the most specious honesty into that of the most hardened effrontery, and the good pastor immediately wrought out a little theory as he observed how close was the connection between the two. The *Disponent* was a hardened brute, and that of the worst sort— one that could conceal his passions ; for he answered not a word —deliberately strode up to the chair to reclaim his bridal gifts, swept up the finery under his arm, threw a look of malice at the bystanders, and left the room.

CHAPTER II.

THE hour for morning service was now approaching. The church, which stood within a few yards of the *Pastorat*, was a great ugly building, built only for the use of worship, and not for its symbol, and down the one trodden tract, which looked like a deep furrow in the monotonous field of snow around, came pouring the congregation in irregular procession. The little rude sledges drawn by small shaggy horses, and holding sometimes a whole family party, sometimes only one indolent man, glided swiftly along, passing whole rows of pedestrians, chiefly women and girls, who paced nimbly and lightly one after the other in perfect silence. The men were mostly clad in sheepskins—the wool inside—their own wool lying on their shoulders in various states of entanglement; some in heavy strands, others with every hair standing on end with the frost, but all looking very warm and very picturesque, as most dirty things do! The women were more striking. The high, stiff, helmet-like caps they wore on their heads were covered with ample folds of white linen, which passed in a low bandage over the forehead, and in graceful oval lines down the cheeks, till, with their brown woollen upper garments, something like a short pelisse, covering all the gay striped petticoats underneath, they might have passed for some humble religious order. Though many had come a considerable distance, yet the keen clear air had braced their steps and coloured their cheeks, and the groups wore that certain Sunday-look of freshness and peace so grateful to the mind both in reality and association.

When the sledges had discharged their loads at the church gate, the next business was to stow them in some way near it, and soon they stood, packed together, as closely as the carriages may be seen at the height of the season before some fashionably attended morning concert ; the vehicles differing not more than the object they were assembled for.　Many of the owners left their sledges to the discretion of their horses, and the little animals drew close together, and some of them rubbed noses most affectionately, while others sneered and tried to bite, in a manner very much the reverse.

Meanwhile, most of the women and children had entered the church, the men remaining in groups, talking in their babbling monotonous tones.　Soon it was apparent that some new and very piquant anecdote was going the round of the assemblage, and knowing looks were given, and white teeth shown from ear to ear, and witty things said—and all particularly pointed at a young peasant, conspicuous for his fine figure and face, who seemed not to take them particularly amiss.　But now the pastor, in his rusty black Geneva robe, was seen emerging from his house, passed through them with many a kind look and word, and the congregation thronged into church.

Anno was already at her place, her betrothal garments covered up with the customary brown robe, and looking now very much like all the other girls around her, only that she was far prettier, and even prettier to-day than usual.　Full in front of her stood that same young peasant, erect and broad-shouldered ; and though Anno was so attentive to the service that no one in the church ever saw her lift her head from her hymn-book, yet somehow she managed to ascertain that her *vis-à-vis* was in full possession of the events of the morning, and no little satisfied with the share he had taken in them.　How it had all got out we do not pretend to say, but the pastor's kitchen was the very centre of gossip, and the good old gentleman himself not over-discreet. We need hardly say that this was the *Disponent's* successful rival, and nobody who had once seen him could wonder or regret that he was so.

Mart Addafer, though surnames are superfluous in Lettish peasant life, was truly a fine creature.　He had as handsome a person and as generous a soul as ever caught the eye and won the heart of woman.　He was so different from his poor, low-minded, dull, fellow-peasants, that it seemed unfair to both to place him among

them.   But the difference was not of a kind to unfit him either
for his country or his countrymen.   He had only all the happier
qualities of the Livonian nature in a higher degree—none that
were foreign to it.   He was neither sharp, nor quick, nor am-
bitious : but he had the sound moral feeling, the plain strong
sense, the noble patient courage, and the sweet gentle temper,
which, even under the cruellest want and oppression, are never
quite obliterated from a Livonian breast.   The same might be
said of his person.   He was just the type of the national good
looks ; his figure unstunted by misery, and his face undebased by
intemperance.   He had the fresh ruddy complexion, the brown
curling hair, the open brow, the clear blue eye, and then such a
beautiful set of teeth as might alone have undertaken to redeem
the ugliest countenance, and which the lightest heart and the
sunniest temper were always showing.   Altogether Mart was
one of those happily constituted beings whom it is refreshing to
meet with in any rank, not because they are so much better than
their fellows, but because their excellence seems to be more
spontaneous, starting, as it were, straight from the heart-roots of
their own nature, without any intervening foundation of error,
struggle, suffering, or discipline.   Such as he was day by day and
year by year, he seemed to have been created—goodness his
nature, labour his pleasure, and life his enjoyment.   Mart was
truly *simple*.

It would indeed have been a pity had anything come between
Mart and Anno.   She was not his equal in mind or sense, indeed she was still too young to know what she was ; but she was
true-hearted, affectionate, and industrious, and the mistake that
had discovered her preference evidently gave too much pleasure
to Mart for any one to doubt of his.   Before he left the churchyard he received many a sly intimation that the same old mother
could easily be induced to carry another message to the same
house, only taking due care that there should be no further mistake, and also many a grave warning not to have anything to do
with a girl who might be pretty, but whose father was poor and
idle, and who could only give her the clothes on her back, and
not the usual stock of those.   But Mart went his own way; he
wanted no old hag to invent for him what was not true, or to
mystify what was ; he did not care a straw whether Anno had

the usual outfit of clothes or whether she had any at all, but he strode away at the utmost speed of his active limbs, overtook the old man and his daughter before they had gone a werst on their road, and, ere they separated, had in every way rectified and repaired the mistake of the morning.

Mart had no one to oppose his choice—he stood almost alone in the world—he had never had brothers nor sisters—both his parents were recently dead, and only an old grandmother remained, who lived with him, and whom he supported with great respect and tenderness. His father had been, like old Tonno, Anno's father, poor and idle, but also, like Tonno and many others in this part of the world, idle chiefly because he was poor—because he had seen himself gradually go down in the world under a set of hard laws and a perpetual change of masters, in spite of his best efforts to recover himself, and because after a while he had lost both heart and strength to renew them. But though he had left the fields which he held on the estate in a miserably exhausted state, and the buildings he and his cattle occupied in the most dilapidated condition, yet they were no longer the same now. Mart had thrown the whole weight of his cheerful spirit and his vigorous arm upon them, and was already known as one of the most steady payers of his rent, and the most punctual performers of his allotted days of service (the old *frohn Dienst*) upon the estate. He was not rich, nor hardly to be called easy, as peasant life goes, in his circumstances, but he was a rising man; and this description of suitors we recommend to young ladies far more than those who have ready-made fortunes to offer.

Under these circumstances there did not seem much occasion for a very long courtship. Anno's dowry would not increase with the delay of the marriage-day, nor Mart's industry diminish with the speedy celebration of it; on the contrary, he assured her that he felt much more tempted to waste time while there were eleven wersts between them, than he should do when she was under his own roof. But whether this was most true or most ingenious, we must leave.

One afternoon, therefore, Mart dressed himself out in his Sunday best, and, accompanied by another peasant, a pale, unhappy looking man, the very antipodes to himself, mounted his cart, for spring had just burst out, and took the road for old

Tonno's dwelling : first, however, having stowed into the vehicle some bundles carefully wrapped up in linen. The road led through several wersts of wood, in which Mart's house stood, and then past the baron's residence, and all the retinue of farming buildings, stables, and outhouses, all built in the same style, with which, as is the fashion in Livonia, the house was surrounded. These were all very heavy, and ugly, and in wretched bad taste, but to Mart's eyes they were beautiful ; and as he looked upon them, and reflected that the owner of all this pomp and splendour —the being who had a right to live in that great rambling house, with all his farming buildings directly under his nose—was voluntarily spending his time and money in a foreign land, Mart felt that this was one of those mysteries of the human heart which his own could not comprehend. The next object that caught his eye was a smaller house, about two wersts off the *Hof*, or baron's residence, and built somewhat in the same style, but this was much more really pretty ; it stood picturesquely with trees behind and above it, and a clear stream before, which gave a still prettier picture of the same thing, only reversed. Then the house was built of stone and painted yellow, with a copper roof painted green, and it had four sash-windows, and a wooden porch, and altogether Mart felt that this was a residence more enviable still.

It was the *Disponent's !* Mart had not passed that way since the day that Anno had declined becoming its inmate and mistress. We will not say that this was so great a mystery to Mart's mind as the last he had tried to solve ; he felt his heart was worth any *Disponent's* house any day, though a modester one never beat ; but still the thought that Anno had given up a yellow stone house, with a green copper roof, and sash-windows, and a porch, and numberless treasures beside, all for him, brought with it an overwhelming feeling as if he could never adore her enough ; and he urged on the little willing horse, and saw and thought of no more houses until he reached that in which his *Einokenne* (only one) dwelt.

This was not a very tempting domicile. It was built on the borders of a large morass, on which the waters of the winter's snow still stood, and which spread also over the few stony, bare-looking fields which composed Tonno's allotted tenure. The house was of wood, old and dark, with a high bristly back of dilapidated thatch hanging down low over two little pig's-eyes of windows, which seemed adapted for anything but the admission of light. The low log walls were stained and rotten, some of the timbers were warped and sunk, and it looked altogether a structure which a spark might set on fire, or a puff blow down. But all around was clean and tidy ; the recent sweeping marks at the low door looked, it is true, as if they expected a guest, but two long stripes of linen bleaching close by, and a numerous brood of hens and chickens chuckling over them, showed that Anno's care had commenced before the present occasion.

As the little cart drove up to the house, not a creature was visible. But soon old Tonno's rough grizzled head appeared from beneath the low door-stall ; he looked very knowing and shrewd, but affected great surprise at their coming, and asked them what they wanted.

"I 'll tell you what I want presently," said Mart, with a significant air, as if he wanted to coquet with the approaching merriment, at the same time tugging away at the shafts to unloose his little horse. "I 'll tell you presently. A fine day, Tonno."

"A very fine day," answered Tonno : "how does your rye come on ?"

"Capitally well," said Mart ; "but I want a pretty bird to help me to peck it, and I hear she has flown in here."

"A pretty bird ! what is she like ? "

"Let me see and I 'll tell you," said Mart.

"Bring out the whole cageful," said his companion ; and Tonno disappeared. Audible sounds of laughter now resounded from beneath the roof, and in a few minutes the old man returned, dragging by one arm a robust peasant girl, all crimson with laughter and shamefacedness.

"Here 's your bird," said Tonno.

Mart pretended to scrutinize the lady, and attempted to take her hand, when he was repelled with that degree of violence which is the approved standard of Lettish modesty. "A very pretty bird," he said, "but she is too shy for me,—you may let her fly."

Again Tonno retired, and again the same laughter was heard, in which Mart thought he caught some tones which set his heart beating. This time Tonno brought forward a weather-beaten hard-worked-looking peasant woman, with the matron's cap on her head, who looked up boldly and good-humouredly at the young man, and seemed to enjoy the joke.

"This is your bird," said Tonno again.

"A very nice bird indeed," answered Mart; "but I suspect she has already got a mate for herself. I shall have my eyes pecked out if I put my head into her cage. No! try again."

Then was brought out a little girl of ten years old, and Mart said she was not fully fledged; and then an old woman, bent with age, and Mart patted her shoulder tenderly, and said he should like her very much, because she would not fly away; but still she was not the right one—with various other witticisms.

"Have you any more birds in your cage?" he inquired.

"No," said Tonno; "the cage is empty now."

"Then I must look for myself;" and leaving the party in a roar of mirth outside, Mart stooped his tall head under the door-stall and entered the house.

What took place then, and where he found the bird, and how he contrived to catch her, we of course do not know. At all events, he was a long time about it, and it was not until old Tonno had summoned them at the top of his voice, and the women had come round and peeped in at the windows, that the parties appeared,—both looking very red, happy, and silly.

Then Mart went in a great hurry, as if to cover some confusion, and brought out the bundles wrapped in linen. Their contents proved to consist of bright handkerchiefs, pretty aprons, and gay ribbons, which each in turn elicited fresh bursts of admiration, and which he hung side by side upon Anno's pretty round arms, till there was not a space left. Then he took a large silver brooch with red glass studs, and put it into one hand, and two silver rouble-pieces, and put them into the other: and having thus laden her with as much as she could hold, he boldly took her head between his great hands, gave her a hearty kiss before all the spectators, and said, "Here's my pretty bird."

As this was felt by all the party to be pretty conclusive, though not necessarily belonging to the ceremony, Tonno now invited them all to enter the house, when, bringing out a bottle of spirits which had been brewed in better days, they all drank to the health of the bridal pair.

We have mentioned the peasant who accompanied Mart in this expedition. His office, according to the ancient rules in these matters, which are strictly kept up among the peasantry, was that of *Brautwerber*, or bride-wooer, though it must be owned Mart had left him but little scope for it. This trust is always committed to a steady married man, usually some near relation of the bridegroom, who serves as spokesman for one who is supposed to be too bashful to speak for himself. It is well, therefore, that on this occasion the bridegroom was not of this description, or he would have found but little help in the *Brautwerber* he had selected ; for Juhann, as we have said, was pale and timid-looking, and as melancholy and silent as his looks bespoke. Nobody wondered at Mart's choice of him on this occasion, for all knew that they were sworn friends, but how they came to be so it was difficult to account for, except by the contrast in their characters. So it was, however. Mart loved the poor, anxious, depressed-looking creature, and he in return would do anything for Mart, and certainly would have undertaken this office for no one else, nor now ,without much persuasion ; also with the conviction, perhaps, that it would prove what we have shown it to have been—a complete sinecure.

It is needless to describe Anno's second visit to the Pastorat, nor how the ceremony of betrothal went off without the slightest interruption or mistake. The good pastor looked at the young couple before him with the deepest interest, read off Mart's honest, open countenance with the most entire satisfaction to himself, and threw into his address a tenderer tone of exhortation and comfort. Altogether this little episode spoke to a set of feelings in his breast which, in the exercise of his avocation, generally lay dormant. He had long come to that conviction to which all actively benevolent persons do, or should arrive, that the disappointment of the finer and more delicate sentiments of the heart is the necessary price you pay for the exercise of charity, especially towards such objects as need it most ; and that, in truth, you are never purely and disinterestedly charitable till you do forego all expectation of their indulgence. He knew too much of the straitening and numbing influence of excessive material want to wonder that the more poetical parts of the human character should perish beneath it. These, he felt, would always start up into life the moment the weight which impeded them was removed; and meanwhile, that the roots from which alone they spring should still preserve their vitality, only furnished him, like a true Christian philosopher as he was (albeit a German), with a further argument for the truth and power of the Gospel he preached. For the Lettish peasant, however abject misery may make him, is still always a believing creature, easily directed to good, bitterly penitent in evil.

Under these circumstances the pastor looked at the young and handsome couple before him with a feeling of almost romantic interest. Disinterested love was a virtue, and happy love a luxury, which he seldom had the pleasure of witnessing among his poor peasantry. He was kindly interested in all who came before him, but there was that in the history, appearance, and tenderness of Mart and Anno in which he could positively sympathise. He felt that he had not given this woman, as he gave too many others, merely to be a slave's slave, but to become the cherished wife of an honest, upright man.

We shall be thought to have laid far too much stress upon the form of betrothal, considering that that of marriage has still to come. But, in truth, among this primitive people, both the ceremony that precedes it and the festivities that succeed to it are felt to be of far more importance than the wedding ceremony itself. This latter the Lettish peasant appears to go through with simply because the law requires it. The solemnity of the occasion to him is over—the rejoicings still to come. Generally speaking, therefore, he appears at the church without any holiday signs upon him, in his every-day working garment, and unattended, save by the necessary witness. As for taking his wife home to his own dwelling after the ceremony is over, this is an indecorum no Lettish peasant would dream of. No! the wedded couple separate at the church door, and go their way, not to meet again until the day appointed for their own

national modes of merry-making. As for Mart and Anno, however, they are suspected of having been guilty of very great
breaches of etiquette, for he was known to have walked the
greater part of the way home to Uxnorm with her from church,
and a cart and horse very much like his were decidedly seen
there next evening.

CHAPTER III.

On the appointed day there was an early meeting of friends and
relatives at Mart's house.   His invitations had been most liberal
—he was a universal favourite—the day was fine, and one little
cart-full of gay wedding guests rattled up to the door after another.   Preparations for plentiful feasting had been going on for
some days previous, under the superintendence of the old grandmother, a venerable, mild-looking old dame, who went tottering
about in a new apron of the brightest red, yellow, and green
that could be found—Mart's particular gift for the occasion.
The house was swept clean, and strewn with fresh sprigs of
spruce-fir ; the wooden barrels and drinking vessels were all as
fresh and as white as the running waters of the stream could
make them ; Mart's old dog, a fine creature, in size and colour
like a lioness, kept wagging his tail without ceasing ; the cocks
and hens retreated up to the rafters of the roof, and there stood
and crowed perpetually, and every living thing seemed in good
humour.
    Conspicuous among the arrivals were two smart young pea-
sants, who looked particularly full of bustle, importance, and
facetiousness, and seemed in some respects to take the direction
of matters even over the bridegroom himself.   These were the
Marshals—a species of *best men*—whose office is also very ancient
and important, and who now reminded Mart of what he was all
ready to remind them, namely, that it was time to fetch the
bride.   A little procession of carts, therefore, set out, headed by
the Marshals and including most of the male guests, and Mart,
of course, among them ; while one cart in particular, Mart's
own, decked up with boughs and driven by the *Brautwerber*,
was evidently destined to bring back the prize.   The hour was

still early, the roads were good, and they met with no incident on the way.

Arrived at Uxnorm, where they found also a cluster of guests awaiting them, the Marshals alighted first, and entered in the name of the bridegroom to demand the bride. They were not long about this proceeding, or Mart would soon have been after them, but reappeared in a few minutes, followed by, rather than leading, the young girl. Anno was apparently in her usual dress, her tight-fitting woollen garment covering all decorations beneath; but her pretty head was quite bare, her maiden circlet had been left behind, and the matron's cap had not yet taken its place. The door of the house was low and wide—the slim figure, and modest, tender head, stood in full relief against the dark interior, and as she lingered, unconsciously perhaps, on the threshold, and looked back one moment, Mart's manly heart swelled with that exceeding gratefulness which seems at once to change a selfish passion into a holy duty. The father showed himself not—he stayed behind. This is the etiquette at a Lettish wedding. The man fetches his wife unaided by his parents,—the woman leaves her home uncompelled by hers; each is free.

But at that moment etiquette was far enough from Mart's thoughts. The instant her foot quitted her father's threshold he was at her side, lifted rather than helped her into the cart, and, in defiance of all rule and custom, seized the reins himself, and sprung in after. In vain did the *Brautwerber* meekly expostulate, and the Marshals imperiously dictate—Mart was in full possession, and in such a state of uproarious happiness that there seemed to be no access to his understanding by the usual channels. The little horse knew his master, and set off at full speed, and all the anxiety of the Marshals was now directed to prevent his taking the lead in the procession, which would have been the climax of impropriety. This they managed to avert after a short race, when Mart, having effected his aim, dropped contentedly behind them, and the little horse was left very much to please himself.

The day was now up; the procession, swelled by Anno's bridesmaids and relatives, cut a most imposing figure, and the Marshals were anxious to exercise their privileges, namely, that of making every other vehicle on the road turn off for them.

The first they met were humble peasants like themselves, who were as willing to observe the custom as they were to exact it, and who drew off immediately to the side, and waved their caps as the party passed. A werst or two farther on, however, a private barouche was seen approaching—four spirited horses full in the middle of the road, as if they would run down all that opposed them—a long-bearded coachman on the box as firm and immoveable as the engine on a steam-carriage. Now was the time for asserting their rights. The *Brautwerber*, timid man! was all for relinquishing them, but the Marshals had warmer blood in their veins. They knew well enough what it was to turn off for their haughty masters, to stick in the road-side mud, or struggle in the road-side drift, while the Baron's carriage rolled by without yielding an inch, not to make the most of such a rare opportunity for retaliation. Pulling and chucking, therefore, at their little horses, who, from the force of habit, had already begun to turn their heads patiently aside, they drew them close together, and supported immediately behind by Mart himself, who, in his turn, encouraged the procession to keep their places, they presented a firm phalanx. On came the four horses sweeping along, the coachman started into life, shook the whip which hung upon his wrist, and discharged a mouthful of Russian oaths at the body. A concussion now seemed inevitable, when a broad, good-humoured face leant forward from the barouche, saw the state of the case in a moment, and discharged a very similar volley at the coachman in return. The carriage instantly swerved to one side. This was quite enough. Every cap flew off, every face expanded, and there was not one of the party who would not have been willing to drive their carts into a ditch for that same good-humoured face another time.

On they went more merrily than ever, undisputed lords of the road, ready to defy the Autocrat himself, if one of his meteoric courses had led him in that direction. Their way now turned off from the high road towards the mansion and farming buildings we have spoken of before. The great mansion with its front of five-and-twenty windows lay in the distance, and close on one hand was the *Disponent's* with its four, two to the south, and two to the east, with the sun full upon the yellow walls and green roof brighter than ever.

" A pretty house," said Mart.

" *Vegga illos* "—very pretty—whispered his companion.

" Shall I drive you there, Anno? " he said, with a sly expression.

" Yes, when you are *Disponent*," answered Anno. This was said so livelily, and with such a look up into his face as she had never ventured on before, that it was no wonder that Mart took occasion to whisper something particularly confidential ; on which down went Anno's head low into her lap, and Mart's almost as low after it. Nothing, indeed, but the singularity of such a position could have prevented the young couple from seeing a one-horse vehicle, of a kind of droschky shape, which was advancing rapidly. As it was, they were first roused from the conviction of there being no other individuals in the world but their two selves, by the harsh voice of the *Disponent* himself summoning the Marshals to turn off the road.

Now there is something in the very place and person of a *Disponent* particularly odious to a half-civilized peasantry, like these we are describing, who have still too much of the serf in them to dream of questioning the authority of their masters, but too much also of the freeman to bear the tyranny of a class possessing all the mischief of their master's power, without the *prestige* of their position. It is invariably the *Disponent* of an estate to whom all the misery and misrule upon it are to be traced. Their interest is equally served by the negligence of the proprietor and the ignorance of the peasant, and the one is usually misled and the other misrepresented as best suits their mercenary purposes.

Setting aside the personal hatred in which Ian was held, it was sufficient that he was a *Disponent* for them to rejoice in this opportunity for exercising their short prerogative. Even the *Brautwerber* shook his matted locks and brandished his whip in signal of resistance, and it was evident not an inch would be yielded by his consent. Mart, however, was quiet. His blood mounted and his eyes dilated like an ancient Barsark, as he overheard the swaggering commands and Jack-in-office abuse which the fellow levelled at the party. But Anno was frightened, and as he put his arm round her, he felt that he was not quite so free to fight his quarrels with one who could work him so much good or ill, as he had been a few weeks before.

Besides, he really bore the *Disponent* no unkindness. It is easy and sweet to be generous when you are happy, and Mart felt that Ian's mortification had been his triumph. The Marshals, however, were exceedingly pugnacious. They belonged to another estate, which did not come under his jurisdiction, and they levelled the best Lettish slang at him at the top of their voices. The shaking of harness and the creaking of wheels was now heard, and the parties stood up in their respective vehicles, as if eager to throw their grappling-irons. There is no saying what might have ensued, when one of the Marshals gave the *Disponent's* horse a cut across the face, which made the poor animal turn sharp aside with a suddenness his master could not stop—down went the wheel into a ditch—the whole party swept past with cheers and groans of derision, and a stout voice called out, " Where's your wife, Ian? We'll turn off for you when you bring her home."

This was the crowning triumph of the day. They now entered the little forest-road in which there was no further chance of obstruction, and mending their pace, drove on for some time in silence. Then they broke out into a low monotonous chant, which, though far from musical in itself, rang pleasingly through the thicket of irregular trees which led to Mart's house, and announced their approach before they themselves became visible.

Anno had never seen Mart's dwelling before.

" It is not so beautiful as Ian's house," said Mart in a low voice.

" *Illos küll*"—beautiful enough—answered Anno, in a still lower.

The cart now stopped at the low wide door, which was crowded with guests awaiting their arrival, and the married lovers' *tête-à-tête* was over. The Marshals, elated with their late successes, were all on the alert to fulfil their parts. · The gloves suspended to the shafts, which are supposed to bring good luck to whoever reaches them first, were eagerly snatched : the bride was lifted from the cart at one bound on to a sheepskin extended before the door, to signify that the way through life was henceforth to be soft to her feet—a type, alas ! to which there is no reality, at least not under a Russian government ! The *Brautwerber* strewed corn before her, in emblem that abundance was to follow her to her new home, and thus she was carried in noisy triumph over her husband's threshold. There, surrounded by the women who had remained behind, and propped in a rude high-backed chair, sat Liso, Mart's grandmother, ready to receive the new comer.

This was their first meeting, and the old dame threw a searching and a solemn glance on the slight girl, in whom she saw at once the maiden her grandson had wooed, the bride he had betrothed, and the wife he had married. Anno bent involuntarily before her, and not a word was exchanged, as, slowly rising and coming forward, the old woman took a high stiff cap made of white silk and placed it on Anno's pretty head. Voices had been loud, and faces merry, but all were now hushed and serious, for this simple ceremony went to everybody's heart.

The meeting between youth and age is at all times a touching sight and an impressive lesson, telling us what the one has been and the other must become. The very difference between them disposes the mind to reverse more than to compare—to put the aged back, and the youthful forward. Anno's head trembled with girlish timidity, old Liso's shook with infirm age; yet both were only separated by that time which time itself would unite.

When the cap had been slowly adjusted, the grandmother again gave a glance at Anno, and in a shrill, distinct voice repeated this ancient form of words which belongs to the ceremony :

"Forget thy sleep.—Remember thy youth.—Love thy husband." Accompanying each sentence with a slight stroke of Anno's cheek. Then turning to Mart,

"Ah! my son, my son ;—you are a good man ; you have chosen a beautiful wife ; I know she will be a happy one." Then addressing Anno, "He has been always good to an old grandmother, will he not be good to a young wife! I hope you are worthy of him."

"Grandmother—*pai* (good) grandmother!" said Mart, in a tone of expostulation ; but Anno stood upright with modest self-possession ; and, taking Mart's great brown hand in hers, she kissed it with wifely reverence. Then going round to all her new relations and guests, she begged their affection, as is the custom, and kissed their hands—not even the *Brautwerber's* little puny boy of three years old was omitted. And Mart's eyes followed the movements of that new white cap with exultation, for he felt that the face beneath must win all hearts. Finally, she patted old Karria Pois, who sat gravely by the grandmother's side looking on, and who lifted his broad forehead under the pressure of her hand, and raised his large gentle eyes to her, with as affectionate a look of welcome as any she had received. Then placing herself next Liso's chair, she quietly stooped for a little wooden footstool which had been pushed away, and placed it beneath the old woman's feet, as if by this simple action to show that her course of filial service was begun.

In the estimation of most present, especially of the women, the placing of the cap was by far the most important ceremony that had occurred, and certainly Anno's own feelings inclined that way. She had listened to the exhortation at her betrothal with awe, and received the marriage benediction with wonder; but there was something more than both in the touch of that aged hand on her cheek, and in the pressure of the cap on her brow, which made her feel that now indeed she was a wife.

The male guests now all turned out again; and Anno mingled with the other women in preparing the meal, and delighted old Liso's heart by her evident neatness and skill.

This meal, which answered the purpose of breakfast and dinner both, consisted of but few dishes, and those of a primitive kind. There was a whole row of wooden vessels full of sour milk, with cream an inch thick upon it—a national and most delicious dish, which the daintiest palate need not despise, but which requires the richness of a Lettish pasturage and the heat of a Lettish summer to prepare. Then there were plenty of pickled *Strömlin* —the anchovies of the North—which in times of average plenty form the chief article in the daily food of the peasantry; with tubs full of hot smoking crayfish, lobsters in miniature, which abound in the streams of this country, and are much in request for the tables of the upper classes. Of substantial loaves of fermented rye-bread of course there was a great provision, varied by another and lighter kind called *Seppig*, being the same unfermented, which served for cake. All these solids were duly counterbalanced by a profusion of strong beer, or what in other lands would come under the denomination of ale, the produce of

Mart's own field and hop-garden: while two of those peculiar shaped bottles which seem predestined to much the same purpose all over the world, raised their slender throats from out of their big bodies, full of the colourless dew of a finer and stronger distillation—of which, by the way, Northern heads and stomachs can bear more than any other nation.

The meal was conducted with great propriety; the young couple sat together for the first time, and the Marshals did the honours and plied the guests, who were very quiet and silent, as hungry people with a full board before them usually are. On this account perhaps this meal is not looked upon as the chief entertainment. The company is supposed to eat from simple appetite, and not from epicurean enjoyment. Other ceremonies had to be performed, and even among this rude people there is a feeling against revelling in the day-time. The daylight is another thing, and not to be avoided at a season when the night is only a paler day about three hours long.

Accordingly, having satisfied their appetites, they left the benches and again dispersed—the men smoking their pipes and lounging at the door, or sleeping upon the bank of the stream in the sun, occasionally exchanging some facetious remarks with the women and girls cleaning the wooden vessels, as they passed backwards and forwards to the stream. Anno, however, never appeared from within; and Mart, who neither slept nor smoked, was frequently missing from without.

During this *entre acte* old Tonno, with a few other decrepid worthies, arrived. By rights he should not have come till the next day; but Mart was determined to curtail the time of festivity, and to cram every possible rite and every possible hospitality into a shorter time than usual. Anno blushed up under her very cap as she saw her father, who, according to a customary witticism, pretended not to know her in this costume.

His arrival was the signal for another national observance of more importance to the worldly welfare of the young couple than any that had preceded it. The Marshals now started up into activity, gave three or four loud discordant whoops to rouse those who slept, and summon those who had wandered, and soon assembled them all in a numerous body before the house.

It was altogether a pretty scene. The sun had begun to

decline from its long-held height in the heavens, and the sloping shadows of the trees fell over the long straight roof and low walls, and played and quivered among the crowd assembled at the door; which, with the bright costumes of the women, the dull coarse garments of the men, and the uncouth figures and faces of too many of them, together with the rough benches and tables, and picturesque wooden vessels scattered around, looked like some northern Ostade's Village-feast.

The *Brautwerber* now came forward, and, taking a small parcel from his pocket, shook out what might at first sight have been safely taken for some variety of national flag, but which the ladies present instantly recognised to be the newest and most fashionable description of apron. Then, diving for Anno, who was ensconced behind everybody else, he brought her forward, and with some pretended, and quite sufficient real awkwardness, succeeded in tying it up round her short but slender waist. Then the Marshals came up; each took a corner of the apron, and, examining it attentively, shook their heads and said, " This is not a good apron."

" What ails it ?" inquired the *Brautwerber*.

" It 's an old rag," they answered; " there 's a hole in it."

" Perhaps this will mend it," rejoined the *Brautwerber*, and threw in a silver half-rouble.

" That 's a good beginning, but it will want more yet. Hold tight, Anno ;" and they each threw in a silver coin, declaring that the hole was bigger than they had thought, and that it would take a good deal to stop it. Then each guest in turn drew near, and flung in their offerings, which fell heavy or light according to the means of the giver. Long the little silver shower continued, while Anno stood and bent her head gracefully, and whispered " *Olge tervis* "—thank you—as each coin fell.

The Marshals now again approached, and declared there were several more holes they had not observed at first—great ones— and again each cast a mite into the growing treasury. Their example was followed with increased alacrity. In vain Anno repeated " *Olge tervis*," and Mart interposed with " *Küll, küll, ea küll* "—enough, enough, quite enough; the gifts continued. The fulness of the bride's apron is as much the test of the popularity of the bridegroom as of her own ; and Mart's warm heart and strong arm had rendered too many services to his neighbours not to be requited on such an occasion as this, when all purse-strings are supposed to hang very loose.

Nor were their donations confined to the coin of the realm ; a hank of fine white wool was thrown in by one hand, and a bunch of shining flax by another ; then a roll of stout homespun linen, and a piece of coarse woollen cloth, and ribbons, and woollen gloves, and a little bit of coarse lace, and various other articles of female use or luxury. Then a measure of fresh eggs was placed down on one side of her, and a small tub of salt butter for winter luxury at the other ; and suddenly a new spinning-wheel appeared in front ; and a crazy old basket, out of which peeped several chickens' heads ; and, lastly, a tottering calf was driven up, till Anno was fairly surrounded with objects of household wealth, and stood in the midst like the Goddess of Abundance. Then more and more was heaped upon the apron, till either the bride's arms or the apron-strings seemed in danger of giving way ; and at last the Marshals pronounced it to be fairly mended, and not a hole more discernible.

But now old Liso hobbled forward, and, with her wrinkled face lighted up with a cheerful pleasant expression, turned to the Marshals, and told them they were young men, but still they were very blind ; that even her old eyes could see another great hole, and one which only her offering could repair.

"Daughter," she said to Anno, "all your presents are very beautiful, and your neighbours have made you very rich ; but there is nothing in all they have given you which can mend the holes of human life like this. The time may come when you have nothing left to you of all your worldly goods, but even then, with the blessing of the Lord, you shall find this enough." So saying, she drew forth a Lettish Testament, which looked as if it had had the care and wear of many a year, and laid it top-most on the heap.

Now the apron was actually in danger, and how its contents were not all spilled was really a wonder ; for Anno's arms were in a moment round the old woman's neck ; but Mart's ready hand had seized the load ; and, untying it from Anno's waist, he stood holding it in her stead, and looked on with glistening eyes.

We pass over the concluding scenes of the wedding festivities, which had far more noise and less meaning in them than any which have hitherto been described ; and which lasted so long, that Anno longed to lay aside her heavy new cap, and Mart to dismiss his guests. They were not, however, to be let off so easily. The jollity ceased, it is true, with the setting of the sun, but rose again the next day, though not so early as he. Then they adjourned to old Tonno's house, as is the custom, and then returned to Mart's, and, in short, pretty well ate and drank up the value of what they had presented, before they left the young couple to themselves to begin what are called the realities of life.

CHAPTER IV

IF ever these same realities, as they are inappropriately called only because they are disagreeable, promised to fall lightly on any human heads and hearts, it was on the present occasion. Mart and Anno were both so young and cheerful and pious. They had injured no one, and everybody liked them. Neither did they expect a life of ease, but both were willing to work, and it was a pleasure to work for each other. And then there was that good old woman, the wisdom of whose age seemed only to encourage the trustfulness of their youth. For though there might be hard seasons, and bad harvests, and cruel masters, of which she had had her full share, yet Liso knew that the world would come to an end sooner than the blessing of God fail in His own time and His own way upon one who had cherished an aged parent as Mart had done her.

The summer days flew quickly by; one of the little attentions of Mart's short period of courtship had been to plant a corner of one of his fields with flax for Anno's use, and the plentiful return now showed that no common labour had been bestowed. Otherwise the harvest was far from good, and some grumbled who always grumbled, but some also shook their heads who were not given to despond.

But the truth is, that on most estates in this country, and especially on those left to the tender mercies of a *Disponent*, it is only in the best of harvests that the peasants are kept above want; bad times they can never afford to meet. Mart, however, had not much to fear. He had some little provision for the future, and also he had no debts either in corn or labour to pay, as too many have; and this enabled him to give all his spare summer time to improving his fields. He was a tenant upon the

ancient tenure, giving three days' work himself and his horse to
the proprietor of the estate, as a weekly rental for the portion he
cultivated for his own maintenance, besides a certain allotment of
corn, linen, fowls, and eggs.   This tenure falls very hard upon
the ignorant and careless peasant, especially since the so-called
act of enfranchisement has relieved the upper classes from all responsibility for his welfare and support, and retained their full
authority over his labour.   A single man's work for three days
in the week during the short Russian summer can hardly cultivate sufficient land to maintain him and his family the year
round.   Then, besides the portion of corn for the landlord,
another, never grudged, be it said to their honour, goes to the
clergyman ; while a third is exacted from him to put into what
is called the *Bauerklete*, or peasant's granary ; in other words,
to contribute to a fund of corn against the time of scarcity ;
which fund, from mismanagement, theft, or fraud, is too often
found low or empty when most required.

It is true the peasants are frequently improvident, lazy, and
inclined to avoid their quota of labour, but still their sufferings
arise quite as much from the overreaching of their rulers as
from any short-comings of their own.

Mart's work was by no means light this summer.   He was
willing and active as usual, but, do what he would, nothing went
right.   The most fatiguing labour was always allotted to him ;
all he did was pronounced ill done ; his feelings were insulted
with unjust suspicions ; his temper was tried with abusive language ; and Liso and Anno saw him often return to them after a
long day's absence with a weariness which seemed to be as much
of the mind as of the body.

Anno had her suspicions as to the causes of all this, but as
long as he did not speak she forbore any allusion, and only endeavoured by womanly tenderness and attention to make his
home-life within compensate for his discomforts without.

Time crept on with rather an increase than a diminution of
this tyranny.   Mart's light heart and generous temper struggled
hard.   It was not the present trial that he minded ; he would
not have cared how his duties were increased or encumbered for
a while, if with the labour of his hands and the determination of
his mind he could have worked them off ; but it was a new feel-

ing for him to have a fear for the future, and this it was which struck the deepest. Not that he was much weighed down; as long as his home was undisturbed and his conscience unclouded Mart could not be unhappy, and his clear whistle was still heard in his field, and his white teeth seen bared with laughter before his house door.

Several weeks had thus elapsed when Mart returned one day from his distant work with an expression of face Anno had never seen before. He was haggard and miserable. He said nothing, however, and sat down mechanically to his evening meal, though it was evident he did not know what was before him. Anno had still too much of the child about her to venture to search the cause for his depression, though enough of the woman to try every way to soothe it. All the little accumulated home news of one day—all the trifles, precious or worthless, according to how they are told, or how they are heard, were raked and scraped together with infinite ingenuity. Poor Mart was both too sweet tempered and too miserable to be impatient, but his heart was not in a word she said. At length, he flung his arms down on the board, laid his curly head upon them, and groaned aloud.

" Mart! Mart! what is the matter?" said Anno, now really frightened beyond all concealment. " Tell me, pray."

" Oh! Anno," said her husband, " we are ruined! Anno, we are ruined! Look here," and he gave her a little scrap of coarse Russian paper with a few words scrawled upon it. Anno could not read writing very quickly, but she saw at a glance what this meant. It was a summons to draw lots at the next recruitage.

" Mart," said Anno, " this is the *Disponent's* doing."

Mart nodded his head in mournful assent. Both had long felt he was their enemy, and both knew too well why. Not a word further was spoken between the young couple for a few minutes, during which Mart sat staring blankly before him, with Karria Pois poking his great nose unnoticed into his hand; and Anno was turning over every imaginable expedient in her mind to remove it.

" We can buy you off, Mart," she exclaimed hastily. " We can buy you off. We'll sell the pigs and the young colt, and even the cows if necessary; and then there's the new corn.

How much does the protection cost?" Mart shook his head, and would have smiled if possible.

"A thousand roubles! Anno—a thousand roubles—think of that! We might just as well try to buy the whole estate at once. All our pigs and cows together would not fetch fifty, and the corn is all wanted, and more than ever now, perhaps. No; there's no buying me off."

But Anno had more than one string to her bow. A new hope had struck her.

"There's the scar on your arm, Mart, from the burn when you saved those children. They take no recruits with personal defects."

Again Mart could have smiled. "No, no, my Anno; that did not hurt me then, and won't help me now. I shall suit very well for their purpose, for all that." In truth, this was a still forlorner hope than the last. There were not many such manly, well-grown figures that went up for examination and measurement, and not many so fine an arm to dip for the fatal lot.

But Anno's inventions were not exhausted. Timidly she said, "Do you think, Mart, that if Liso and I—Liso, you know, with me—were to go and beg Ian to help you off?—He always protected you before."

Mart was now no longer inclined to smile. "Not one word, Anno," he said with haste. "You shall never go near that man; I'd sooner be a soldier fifty times over. No, Anno, that won't do; but I may escape—there are several of us. Go and tell my grandmother; I can't," and he flung out of the door and went deep into the wood.

A sudden joy has always appeared to us a great waste of the materials of happiness, and a threatened evil an equal aggravation of the ingenuities of misery. There is enough in the mere anticipation of certain happiness (humanly speaking) to smooth down many an existing evil, and too much in the dread of possible sorrow to embitter many a surrounding good.

It was a wretched and a heavy period for our young couple which intervened between the day which announced this trial and the day which was to decide it. The weather was splendid —the seed was put well into the ground—every thing in the little household promised well. But promises point to a future,

and their future lay behind a dark barrier. Mart took alternate
fits of listless depression and excessive hard work, and between
the two he shrunk so much that his clothes hung about him as if
he had had an illness. Anno pursued her usual occupations:
the flax was combed, and the spinning-wheel went its round; but
she pined and grew pale, as if in an unwholesome atmosphere.

Not the least part of this trial was that there was nothing to
do, nothing to prepare, nothing to resist. If the worst came to
the worst, there would be always time enough to settle Mart's
few affairs, and meanwhile they had to bear that which is one of
the severest taxes upon the human mind, namely, the living on
in the same external world with a total change of internal
thoughts.

The good old woman was now the greatest blessing to both.
The miseries of the recruiting time were but too familiar to her,
who had lost two sons in the hard service. She knew, better
than the fears of either could imagine, the real evils which the
dreaded lot entailed. But her piety was of that true kind which
can equally bear the passive suspense or the active sorrow;
simply because it bears them with the strength of another.

Each came to her when their hearts were too full to endure
alone, and yet would not burden the other. Mart tried to be a
man to his wife, but he did not mind being a child to his grandmother, and in a true child-like spirit did he receive that pious
advice and comfort which best restored him to the self-possession
of the true man. He now recovered much of his usual bearing.
He was serious and silent, but gentler than ever, and had that
composure of manner which showed internal peace.

Mart had not known at first which was to be the decisive day;
but now he did; and he told Anno that it was to be on the
Wednesday of the following week. To his grandmother, however, he owned that it was fixed for the Monday. But he de-
ceived his wife, feeling that two days' more of suspense in idea
was better than one day of real agony.

On the Sunday they all went to church. Liso did not often
go, on account of her infirmities, but this time Mart wished they
should be all together. A general gloom was spread through
the congregation, for the recruiting season inspires peculiar
horror in the minds of the Lettish peasantry, and all knew that

by that time to-morrow one or more of their number would be
separated from home, and condemned to a service harder than
every other to mind and body, in which there is neither glory
nor pay. Many were in anxiety for their own relatives, nevertheless all eyes turned upon Mart and Anno, as they helped the
infirm woman up the church path, with peculiar pity, for they
felt that theirs was the hardest case.

Mart went straight into the church; he was averse to idle
talk, and also feared the possibility of Anno's being enlightened
as to the real day. He prayed with his whole heart to be enabled
to meet the result of the next day in a right spirit,—by that he
only meant that result he dreaded,—the other alternative he
could trust his heart to bear, and yet dared not trust his heart to
look at. Anno wept in silence, and did not exchange a word
with a creature.

After service was over Mart waited aloof till the congregation
was dispersed, and then, leaving Liso and Anno in the cart, went
to the pastor's house. There in that spirit of complete confidence
which is one of the most beautiful parts of the faith most opposed
in every way to the Lutheran, and perhaps descended from it, he
laid open to the pastor every feeling of his heart: the great
happiness of his past life, and the struggle it had cost him to re-
sign himself to this unexpected trial.

The good old man was much moved. He had heard with
astonishment that Mart was to draw, knowing that his character
as one of the best-doing peasants on the estate had hitherto
screened him. He had no power to help, for the absenteeism of
the young proprietor of this estate took from him many a means
of softening the condition of the peasants. The *Hakenrichter,*
or magistrate of the district, who directed the forms in such
matters, was a coarse, unfeeling man, who suffered no interference
from an inferior, and, like a true Lutheran, looked upon the
pastor especially as one.

Mart told him openly the ill will the *Disponent* had shown
him since his marriage, and the evident hand he had in this
matter; and then begged the pastor's particular protection to
shield Anno from Ian's malice, or from what might be worse, in
case he should be taken. The old man promised all Mart could
wish, and gave him an almost parental blessing; then, feeling

that tears were in his eyes, he smiled with all his might : " Be of good heart, Mart; I have no doubt I shall see you in your place again next Sunday ;" and so dismissed him.

The next morning Anno was still asleep, when Mart rose and went to his grandmother. The old woman was prepared, and the hymn-book had been in her hand since day had dawned.

" Grandmother," said Mart, after a short pause, " my time is come ; I must go. I cannot speak much to you, for I feel more like a weak child than a strong man. But give me your blessing to think of when I put my hand into the jar."

" Oh ! my son," said Liso, " my blessing you have—the blessing of an old mother upon the most dutiful of sons. I could give you nothing better, if I would ; for God will set His own hand to this. Go, then, and be strong in His strength. Think not of your old mother, nor of your young wife, but think only of the Heavenly Father who is ever nigh. They may take you far from us, but they can't take you far from Him."

Mart covered his face with his hands, and the big tear-drops trickled through. Old Liso's voice failed also. " I hoped not to have done this, Mart ; but He knoweth whereof we are made, and I have never shed a tear of sorrow for you before. Go, go ; you have no strength to spare, and I have none to give now, but strength will come when the need is there. Go, and the blessing of a poor old woman be with you."

Mart stood for a moment, then with a peaceful expression he said, " Your words have done me good, grandmother. I can go better now," and he turned to depart, but something lingered yet at his heart ; he came back. " Take care of my Anno, *pai* grandmother ;" and here his voice broke, and he turned away.

CHAPTER V.

THE number of recruits annually required for the Russian army, at the time we are describing, was the same as it had been for several years past.   Poland first, and Circassia since, have drafted severely upon the army, and, independent of all active service, the favourite pastimes of the great drill-serjeant of the empire require a great amount of human life to keep going.   The rate of supply, therefore, since the accession of his present Imperial Majesty, has never been below the average standard of five in a thousand, and occasionally above it.   Taking the population of the empire at sixty millions of souls, which is considerably below their own boasted valuation, and allowing for the numbers being levied alternate years from half the empire, which rule is often encroached upon, this alone allows the Crown a regular provision of 150,000 recruits per annum.   To which may be added those condemned to the service for crimes and misdemeanors,—those, such as all soldiers' children, condemned to it without,—and the odd numbers accruing from Foundling Hospitals, &c.

Such facts as these show not so much the overgrown size of the Russian army, as the enormous expenditure of life at which it is maintained.

Five men between the ages of eighteen and thirty out of a thousand men, women, and children, of all ages, tell severely upon a population.   There are certain conditions which except certain individuals, but no condition can abate the number required.   No three brothers out of a family can be taken, nor the father of three children, unless there be no one else to supply his place. Also the Crown exempts those it cannot use, such as the lame, the blind, and the sick ; also those the proprietor most wants, for which purpose a right of protection is granted him over a certain number of men, according to the size of the estate.   But all this caution and generosity is at the expense of the remaining peasants, the number of whom, after all these subtractions, is reduced to a small amount, and those necessarily of the most able and useful men in the village.

On the present occasion the population on the estate was such as to furnish the Crown with two recruits, and the risk lay between only eight men; nor was it yet decided whether all of these were competent subjects to draw.

These eight men were now gathered together at the great front steps of the baronial residence we have mentioned, being kept under a kind of restraint by six soldiers, whose shabby ill-fitting clothes, and dull, jaded, extinguished looks, were not calculated to encourage, far less to delude, the hearts of those who were now to throw for this same lot.

Mart was there. He had kept too much aloof from all his fellow-peasants to know who were destined to share this day of trial with him, and his eye ran mournfully over the figures of two or three of the most valuable members of their little village community, and fell with the sharpest pang of all upon the poor meagre person and pale face of the *Brautwerber*. Hitherto Juhann had been screened, not from his lack of strength, or for his wife and two little children, but because he excelled in a species of carpentering highly useful on the estate. The power of protection, in the absence of the proprietor, was left to the *Disponent's* discretion, and Mart felt, what was perfectly true, that the crime for which poor Juhann had forfeited it this time was only that of being his friend.

The *Brautwerber* was standing to all appearance the same as ever; his head sunk on his breast, his limbs all nerveless and unstrung. His little boy, who seemed to have inherited his father's meek pale face, was on his hand. Father and child were seldom separated, and he seemed to have brought him out of mere habit. Mart drew close to him. Juhann lifted his eyes to his friend for a moment with a look of utter apathy, or what appeared such, and then raised them no more. They did not exchange a word. Mart's feelings were wrought up for endurance, and he could neither have borne nor given one word of sympathy.

Presently a coarse domineering voice was heard, and the *Dis-*

ponent appeared at the top of the steps and summoned them
to enter. He was in the full swagger of revengeful insolence,
and had his eye fixed upon Mart. But Mart did not look at him ;
at that moment it mattered not who was the author of this bitter
hour. The pity for his comrades had eased that dreadful sense
of pity for himself. To all the summons sounded like a knell,
and firm knees shook, and ruddy cheeks were blanched as they
moved together up the steps, four of the soldiers bringing up
the rear, as if escorting prisoners. Mart perceived that his
friend could hardly drag his limbs along.

"Lean on me, Juhann," he said, and stooped to support him,
when he saw that the child was still on the father's hand.
"He can't go with us," said Mart; "give him me; I'll leave
him below," and he tried to disengage the little hand which the
Brautwerber held tight in his cold clammy grasp.

"Forward," said the soldiers behind.

"Come on," roared the *Disponent* in front. "What's all this
about?—a child! Kick it down the steps."

At this moment one of the remaining soldiers, as immoveable
a machine to all appearance as his comrades, came forward and
said "*Dai*"—give. It was not the word, but the look that
spoke. Juhann let go his hold. Mart lifted up the little thing
above those next him, and the soldier received it kindly in his
arms. This little act refreshed the poor men's hearts for a
moment.

They were now shown through a great bare hall into a side
apartment, which, though spacious and lofty, was close and unventilated, for the dusky double windows had been left standing
the year round. There, upon coarse chairs brought in for the
purpose, for it was dirty and unfurnished, were seated the *Haken-*
richter (a kind of magistrate for the district), and an officer in
uniform ; behind them, at a long desk, several officials, all high
busy examining registers, scrutinizing passports, and scrawling
over a great many long sheets of coarse paper with the stamp of
the Russian eagle at top.

The *Hakenrichter* was a hard-featured, red-haired, thin man,
who looked as if he could be both familiar and unfeeling. He
had served in the army, and retired from it with that stamp of
character which Russian habits engender and Russian laws

protect. He always punished the weaker party, and prided himself on his justice ; he never believed a word from a peasant, and boasted he was never taken in ; he lied with unblushing effrontery, and thought himself clever ; he was fearfully passionate, and called himself frank ; he had no regard for the feelings of others, and fancied himself witty.

The officer was also very skinny and very ugly. He wore a great number of orders, and his uniform showed him to be an aide-de-camp to the emperor. His face, therefore, testified that he could alternately look the tyrant or the slave as circumstances might require, but otherwise no variety of expression was discernible.

Behind the *Hakenrichter* stood the *Disponent*, who was high in his favour, looking, as usual, all honesty to those above him, and all insolence to those below.

Now ensued a scene, the mere mention of which will be description sufficient. The men, with the exception of poor Juhann, were all apparently in health, and free from deformity of limb, though one was small and puny in size. But the Crown is not satisfied with appearances, lest, peradventure, a recruit should be thrust upon it who might require the hospital instead of the drill. Each man, therefore, in turn was subjected to a personal scrutiny, only to be compared in nature and manner with that carried on at slave and cattle markets : prolonged according to the will and pleasure of the judges, and conducted with every aggravation most insulting to the feelings. It is true, the feelings of the generality of the peasants are not very keen or delicate, and it would be surprising if under all circumstances they were ; nevertheless, on more than one cheek there burned the glow of shame, and in more than one eye there lowered a fire of resentment, which boded a day of heavy retribution, however distant, between the oppressed and the oppressor.

At the conclusion of this disgraceful scene, the individual, still in the same state, stepped upon a plank on which was fixed an upright pole with the regulation standard of height, generally below the usual stunted stature of the peasant. It was absurd to measure Mart, who stood almost a foot above it ; but Russian laws must be performed to the letter.

No demur was made by the officer to any of the men hitherto presented ; though, acting as immediate agent for the Crown, he is generally difficult to please. But now the *Brautwerber's* turn was come, who stood last but two on the list. The officer looked up, saw the small and sickly frame, and said laconically, " *Nelza !* "—he won't do. A burning flush of hope came over the *Brautwerber's* face and throat, who had heard enough of Russian to know what this characteristic word meant. The *Disponent* whispered busily into the *Hakenrichter's* great misshapen ear.

" All a sham, *Herr Major*," said the latter personage, turning to the officer. " The fellow has been starving himself on purpose to get off. He never had an hour's illness in his life. There 's not a stronger man on the estate ; he can do the work of three men. The *Herr Major* does not know what rogues these fellows are. All a sham."

These words told with deadly effect ; for the mere suspicion of having disabled themselves in any way for the service is enough to overcome the fact even of their being unserviceable. " *Davolna* "—enough, answered the officer ; " measure him."

Here again another chance of escape seemed to present itself ; the revulsion from that moment of hope had deprived the *Brautwerber* of his little remaining strength. As he stood upon the plank his whole frame sunk together ; his head dropped on his breast, and his height fell far short of the allotted standard.

" Stand up ! " roared the *Hakenrichter*. " Pull him up."

The soldiers tried to raise him, but the nerveless, unstrung, and bare body slipped through their grasp, and collapsed lower than ever between them. The *Disponent* hastened round with a brutal expression in his eye. A stout stick was in his hand, with it he struck the defenceless man a violent blow. The poor creature started up like a goaded horse ; the soldiers jerked up his head ; it touched the required point for one moment, and then sunk again.

But this was enough. He was ranged aside to lot with the others. Mart had started forward to his assistance, but had been bellowed back by the *Hakenrichter ;* for one of the acquirements of the Russian service is to raise your voice to passion's loudest pitch in all intercourse with inferiors ; and Mart went back, drawing his breath through his teeth. He forgot his own trials, but he suffered tenfold in his poor friend.

Another man followed, and then the last of the eight. He was a sleek-looking fellow, who had from the beginning shown no anxiety. He now went through the appointed ceremony with alacrity, and stood before his judges sound and straight in limb, and those more encumbered with flesh than any which had gone before.

" He won't do," said the *Hakenrichter*, with a peculiar expression of face at his military colleague. The officer looked up with a peculiar expression in return. This was all sufficient for the *Hakenrichter;* he now went on more boldly. " He is deformed," he said. The officer scrutinized the man with the most serious air. " The deformity is internal," said the *Hakenrichter*, " which is always of the worst kind. Will the *Herr Major* take the medical certificate ?" and he handed him a paper. The gentleman addressed gave a glance at its contents, and then thrust it into his pocket.

" He is deformed ! " said the officer with the regular word-of-command tone ; and all the pens behind him went quicker than ever. " Deformed inside. Let him go." And the soldiers carried him out. The man was the *Hakenrichter's* cook, and the certificate a bank-note.

After all this business was over, which occupied hours in reality, however brief in description, there ensued fresh copying of registers, noting down of names, describing of persons, and other devices for securing the chief ends of Russian law, viz., the waste of time and consumption of paper. Meanwhile the poor men, their numbers diminished and their risk increased, stood by with anxious hearts and haggard countenances, waiting till the mysterious scratching of pens and dusting of sand should come to an end. They did not know that the Crown required to be certified of a man's being deformed inside, on five separate sheets of stamped paper.

At length a jar was brought in by the *Disponent* and placed before the *Hakenrichter* with a little paper parcel. This he opened, examined the cards it contained leisurely before the whole party, as an unfeeling operator would his instruments, counted them, put them into the jar, shook them up, and placed the vessel on a low table. The jar was a common earthen one, the mouth just wide enough to admit the human arm, and too deep for any light to be thrown on its contents. As there were two recruits to be taken, Nos. 1 and 2 were the fatal lot.

There is something repugnant and intolerable to the mind in the thought that the fate of a man's whole life should be made dependent on the choice of a little card. It is less derogatory and bitter to the heart to be made to suffer from the tyranny, caprice, or carelessness of another, than from the apparent results of our own will in a matter where neither reason, knowledge, nor experience can avail. That the Providence of the Almighty is linked with every trifle that befals us, it is our great privilege and duty to believe: at the same time, to be always attaching great ends to trifling occurrences is both unwise and unfeasible, and those who fancy they do so are far more liable to spend their lives in the excitement of a perpetual lottery, than in the composure of a perfect trust. We may approach to draw for a great stake with the firmest conviction that no such thing as chance exists; but still it is more than human to bear in mind that while the hand is shilly-shallying between three or four scraps of paper of the same size, willing without a will, and choosing without a choice, that the God of the whole universe is presiding over the decision. There is nothing in the whole economy of our lives in which He calls upon his creatures to act, even in the most trifling circumstances, without some kind of a reason, in the shape of duty, faith, or experience, to guide them, and it is a wicked system, however decked up with the semblance of fairness, when man obliges his fellow to decide upon a most momentous step without the shadow of one to comfort him.

The men were now all ranged in order, as they had been examined before the table. Mart's figure stood conspicuous above all the rest.

"He'll do for the guards, *Herr Major*," said the *Hakenrichter*, "after six months' drilling." And his chuckle was taken up by the *Disponent* in a loud laugh.

"Come," said the officer impatiently, "*Speschi*—make haste—all is ready."

Perhaps one of the most barbarous features in the scene was the total absence of all the cajolery usual in conscription and enlistment occasions. No attempt was made even to delude these poor fellows in this bitter moment. No one spoke them fair; no one talked of its being a fine thing to serve their Zar and their country. No one thought of interposing the slightest veil between them and the real truth. On the contrary, they were made to feel, in every way that levity and insolence could dictate, that a Russian soldier was a thing too utterly valueless in the eyes of his superiors for them to lighten the anxious countenances before them, for one moment, with the most distant hint to the contrary. All the Crown evidently wanted was the strength of their bodies ; their feelings were to be as little studied as their consent.

They were now all desired to come forward in turn as they were called, put their hands quickly into the jar, draw out a card, and not look at it till all had drawn. This is not always the regular plan, but it suited their judges' ideas of order and discipline, and by this means none would be spared his share of the anxiety.

The first summoned was a short thickset man with a frame of muscular strength, and a wide capacious brow, which was now knit with a fearful expression of determination. He was the father of two children. He came forward with a firm step— put his arm in, drew it out in a moment, and then stood motionless, his hand hanging by his side with the card clenched in it.

The second was a mere awkward peasant, who looked foolish and embarrassed, and laughed as much from excess of boorishness as of fear. But the colour fled from his face as his hand entered the jar, and then returned again in a painful glow behind his tanned and unshaven skin, as he dropped the hand containing his fate by his side.

The third was not remarkable in manner or appearance. He was a spare, long-made man, with reddish hair and common features. His gentle eye and quiet manner might have been taken for the national apathy of mind, for he dipped for the card with a composure which seemed to proceed more from habit than effort. But as he returned to his place a sigh burst from the very depths of his heart, which told of feelings you would have been thankful to have thought him without.

It was now the turn of the fourth to draw. He was quite young —not above nineteen, and had been, from the first, in the most pitiable and abject state of fear. He looked weak in mind, and puny in body—too much so even for his average peasant lot in life—far more for that which not the strongest constitution can stand unimpaired. His name was called, but he held back, the tears running down his cheeks, and burst into loud sobs as the soldiers, by the order of the officer, took him to the table and forced his hand into the jar. But there it lay. The *Haken-richter roared* to him in Lettish ; the officer in Russian ; and then the *Disponent* came forward with his stick. The boy saw the action,—gave a piercing scream,—drew his hand instantly out, and let the ominous card fall on the floor. It fell with the blank side upwards ; the soldiers crammed it into his hand, and he was left to totter back to his place, where Mart's kind voice and arm for a moment lent him support.

But it was now Mart's turn. He had been painfully occupied with the last scene, and it must be owned the strong young man started, and felt his strength depart from him as his name was called. But it was only for a moment. He strode to the table,—laid one great fist heavily upon it to steady himself,—plunged the other into the jar, and fell back to his place with the card in his grasp.

The whole of this proceeding was so rapid, and the lookers-on had been so involuntarily interested to see how this fine-looking fellow would behave—Ian had never taken his eyes from him —that a short pause ensued before the next name was called. It was the *Brautwerber's*, who stood next by Mart, and seemed to have derived strength from his very vicinity. But Mart dared not seem even to look at him now—for he knew how unnerving is the slightest act of sympathy, when strength is being gathered to endure the reverse. But he did steal a glance, and was thankful to see him stand firm, and walk steadily to the table. The arm, however, fell into the jar with effort. Poor man ! it was his last ! he fell back dead fainted, and Mart caught him in his arms. There was no air in that room of torture, with those stifling double windows, and the hot tears, fevered cheeks, and knit brows on which they had thrown light. But there was no time for sentiment. Juhann was laid flat on the floor.

" Keep guard," shouted the officer ; and two soldiers marched up to the head and foot of the pale inanimate figure.

" All sham," said the *Hakenrichter*, without one relenting expression in his hard face. " Has he got the ticket?"

" It is in his hand," said Mart, lifting up the close-shut fist.

" All right," said the *Hakenrichter* ; " it will be a surprise to him when he recovers. Ha, ha!—Go back to your place, fellow,—go on."

Mart drew his ticket out of his breast, where he had thrust it. He would not have anticipated the moment of seeing it for the world, and returned to the melancholy file.

The next man now drew ; his was comparatively the easiest task—he had only to take what was left him.

The jar was now taken to the officer, who looked into it, and gravely pronounced it empty.

Now came the decisive moment. No one could remain indifferent to it, and all eyes were fixed in breathless silence upon the actors in this scene. The *Disponent's* great head looked over the *Hakenrichter's ;* the officials left their desks, and crowded round ; Mart forgot the *Brautwerber*, who lay as before, and even the poor drilled-down soldiers who stood over him turned their heads, though their bodies remained immoveable.

The first man came up and slowly unclenched his fist. It had closed over that hated bit of Russian paper with an iron spring, and never till now relaxed in its grasp. He looked at it a moment, and his face seemed to unlock too, and then he looked at his judges with an expression of open, bold hatred, as if, like Tell, he had had an arrow in store for them in case the lot had fallen on him. He was safe.

The second came up with stooping shoulders and hesitating gait; dropped the card with excess of awkwardness, picked it up, and looked round with a shy, happy laugh. He was safe too.

The plot now thickened for the third. The risk was no longer two to seven, but two to five. He stepped forward; by the expression of his face he seemed fully to have made up his mind for the worst ; but to any possessing the key to such feelings, it would have been evident that it was resignation, not apathy, which supported him. He went up with composure,— looked calmly at the card, and then his face expanded with a smile beautiful and touching to look at, and he closed his eyes in prayer. He was safe.

The fourth was pitiable for his youth and helpless terror ; but his conduct, as we have seen, inspired no respect. It was suspected that he had already ascertained his own fate, for his tears had never ceased, and he now threw down the card, without looking at it, with a feeble and passionate gesture ; then wrung his hands and sobbed piteously. He had drawn the fatal No. 1.

"Take him," said the officer ; and two of the soldiers came forward, and placed themselves on each side, while the poor boy turned his red, swollen face beseechingly from one to the other, as if they could let him off.

Oh, Mart ! it was your turn now. How sick would Anno's heart have been, could she have seen you. His was low enough. He felt himself condemned, and could have put himself at once into the soldiers' hands to avoid the unnecessary anguish of looking at his fate. Over and over again had he rehearsed this moment in anticipation, and determined to raise himself above it with words of prayer and feelings of faith. But he remembered nothing ;—he knew nothing, he heard nothing now except the loud beating of his own heart, through which came the jarring sound of his name like some horrid passage in a dream. He advanced like a desperate man,—paused for a moment—the *Disponent's* eye glared demoniacally upon him—then looked— and leaped high up from his feet. Was it joy or sorrow? Oh ! merciful Heaven ! it was joy, joy,—excess of joy !—his eyes dilated ; his stature expanded ; he took one deep breath after another. Then came a gush of intense religious gratitude, and then a sting of self-reproach. Others were suffering, and had still to suffer.

The *Brautwerber* had meanwhile opened his eyes, and raised himself where he laid.

"Bring him up," bellowed the *Hakenrichter*. Mart cared for no more orders or prohibitions now ; he was at his friend's side, and lifted him as he would have done a child. Juhann turned to Mart with a ghastly smile. "You are safe, Mart ! look ! so am I," and he held up his open hand with the harmless ticket in it. Mart took him with one bound to the table, and displayed the card as if it had been a jewel of inestimable worth. If ever there was a radiant face, it was his. He seemed for a moment not to know there was another creature in the room except Juhann and himself.

He laid both his hands on the *Brautwerber's* shoulders, looked down smiling into his face. "Juhann! Juhann! it's all over. We shall be out of this cursed room soon! It's over—do you hear, man? Oh! those poor fellows. I am ashamed to feel so happy."

The last man's lot is already told. He took up his card.

"Do you know what this means?" said the *Hakenrichter.*

"Yes," said the man with a dogged countenance, "I do. I shan't have to draw again next year."

"No," said the *Hakenrichter;* "but you'll have to draw this;" and the hard-hearted man imitated the click of a musket-trigger. Nobody laughed. "There, soldiers, off with his hair." And the soldiers closed upon him.

The men now crowded impetuously out. Mart and Juhann first. Mart did not seem to tread this earth; he felt as if some horrible operation was over—some weary captivity ended—some fatal spell broken. The common air that met him was balm to breathe. Below the steps was a little crowd of anxious relatives—aged parents, brothers, sisters, wives—who had been awaiting the result for hours; and many a touching scene ensued. But Mark's eyes were fixed on one. The soldier was advancing up the steps,—the little boy toddling by his side; he saw the child in the father's arms, and then turned away with too full a heart.

He was not long left to enjoy such emotions, for by this time the two recruits were brought out, looking the more woe-begone from the complete alteration and disfigurement they had undergone. Their long hair—which many Livonians regard with superstitious care, as if, like Samson, their strength lay in it—had been lopped and hacked away in the most barbarous fashion; this process acting twofold—as a badge of the service, and as a preventive against desertion. A cry of compassion rose from the crowd as they appeared. It was a shocking and a revolting sight. With us the recruit seems instantly to mount in the scale of society; here, they looked like condemned criminals, and felt like them too. Poor fellows! no change in this changeable world can be conceived more total and sudden than that they had just undergone. It was not that they had simply fallen in estate, or altered in condition—their very selves were trans-

E

formed. Home, country, language, and religion—all were gone. They were henceforth to know and feel nothing they had known and felt before; it was as if their souls had migrated into another state.

But the lots had fallen mercifully—the men were both unmarried, and both young. They would each leave a gap in their circle, but neither was the centre of one. Their late companions now gathered round them with earnest expressions of sympathy. One of the recruits had a brother in the crowd who had already gone off to give the intelligence; but the other begged that some one present would undertake this office. His home, or what had been his home, was five wersts off. It was fully that out of Mart's way, but his heart smote him that he should even have waited a moment to see whether another would propose, and he instantly volunteered. He could bear the thought of his poor grandmother's prolonged anxiety, with the knowledge that the cause of it had passed away. As he bounded down the steps he caught the *Disponent's* eye—it boded him no good; but Mart was too happy to take in a thought for the future.

Meanwhile the day passed slowly away with the two women at Sellenküll. Old Liso had that habitual piety which covered all the emotions of her heart with the same garb. She would often say that the trials of the very poor are of the most merciful kind, for that they required from them nothing beyond resignation, patience, and industry; that with all her cares and sorrows, she had never had to hesitate how to act, or been puzzled what to think; but, to use her own expressive language, she had always been able to see straight into herself, and straight up to her God,—and without that, summer all the year round would not make a person happy. An indifferent observer would not perhaps have detected that a heavier weight than usual lay upon her. She sat without the cottage door, at her spinning-wheel. Wordsworth says,—

> "Grief! thou hast lost an ever ready friend,
> Now that the cottage spinning-wheel is mute;"

and truly there is something in that happy medium of the liberty it allows and the attention it requires, which is most soothing to an anxious mind.

Anno was meanwhile actively engaged, and seemed to have chosen this day for a purpose of rather rare occurrence among most Lettish housekeepers—namely, for cleaning her house. Ever since Mart had first received the tidings of recruitage she had been putting her little household in order; and now Mart's clothes were taken out, and brushed with many a sigh;—the old dark wooden boxes, which held their wardrobe, were rubbed;—the wooden utensils, which held their milk and *brei*, or porridge, were washed;—the floor was swept—fir-tips strewn, and then Anno went to the stream—bathed—did up her long hair, and appeared, though not in holiday garb, yet in one perfectly fresh and clean.

The evening sun was declining, the time already long past when Mart might reasonably have been expected. Liso's firmness was now fast giving way; her looks were perpetually wandering up the road which would bring her grandson home for better or for worse, and the least movement or sound in the distance, no matter in what direction, set her withered hand trembling with more than age.

It was well Anno was too much engrossed with her own occupations to watch those of another; for the poor old woman's wheel intermitted terribly in its revolutions. Karria Pois was also watching, as if he knew that something impended of consequence to his master. Time passed on. Liso felt, indeed, what Anno had been spared, but also she felt what the poor girl had to suffer; for her worst fears were confirmed by the delay, and the sight of Mart in the distance between two other figures was all that presented itself to her imagination.

Anno had been seated by her side; but had re-entered the house. Karria Pois now rose, snuffed the air, and set off at a slow trot—then broke into a heavy gallop, and was soon out of sight. The light was fast waning, when a distant figure appeared—one alone! Liso was afraid to take hope to her heart. The figure drew nearer and nearer,—it was Mart, there was no doubt—Mart alone, striding quickly along. The poor grandmother dared hardly look up. But his step was light—and, if that did not speak plainly enough, his glad face spoke plainer still; and, if she still feared to believe what it would now have been torture to relinquish, a few sweet words were whispered in her ear, and the old woman folded her hands, closed her eyes, and communed with her Maker.

Mart entered the house; Anno was busy preparing the evening meal. She had for some days shrunk from his eye, and now she did not look at him as he came in. Mart was positively embarrassed; his heart was bursting with the weight of her joy as well as his own; he flung off his cap, sat down on a bench, fondled the dog, and looked at his wife as she moved to and fro. She was so dejected !

" How beautifully neat you have made everything, Anno ?" Anno only got a sigh in return. " But the rain comes in at that corner of the roof; I must mend it : I'll begin next week."

Anno turned quickly and looked at her husband; there was but little light, but Mart's face was radiant. " Mart !" said Anno, her breath rising into a scream, " Next week !"

" Yes, Anno, yes.—Anno, I am free !" And husband and wife laid in each other's arms.

The first agony of joy was over; all was explained, but they still stood together—the happiest hour of the many happy ones they had spent.

" You see, my *Kasikenne* (my little cat), we are not to be separated. You would not take Ian, and he can't take me."

" We should not have been separated, Mart; I should have gone with you." This was the secret of Anno's patience; for this had she set her house in order.

" But my grandmother ?" said Mart.

" God would have cared for her, as you said He would for me."

" Let's go to her," said Mart.

CHAPTER VI.

THE early winter that followed this autumn was a very trying one; not because it was severe—for severity, whether in temperature or authority, hurts no one, if it be but steady; but, like a real tyrant, it was capricious. To the husbandman of these regions it is always desirable that winter should commence its operations with a good foundation of snow. This laid, as much cold may follow as will; the corn is covered over, and his harvest is secured. But this autumn much rain fell; the waters stood on the low parts of the land, and then came sudden cold, and froze up all the pools, and with them the young corn. Sometimes a curious process of destruction takes place—the blades of young rye are seen just rising above the water; a night of frost spreads a sheet of ice over the surface; a day of thaw succeeds, and the expansion of the ice in melting draws up the plants by the roots, and leaves them floating on the water. Altogether much mischief was done, which the following summer would too surely reveal, and which the summer itself could not repair; and meanwhile a long winter had to be encountered.

Mart's fields stood pretty dry, owing to much extra labour in the way of draining; but old Tonno's, which lay low, and received little more tillage than just sufficed to put the corn into the ground, suffered terribly; and, before snow fell, his fields, and many like his, wore that black, withered look which leaves no hope of life in the plants. It was evident that part of the stock of winter corn must be reserved to sow again in early summer, and thus replace what the season had destroyed; and that stock soon proved to be very inadequate to the regular demands upon it, far less to any extra ones.

The best crops of the preceding summer had been, as we have

said, but moderate in return ; the moderate ones wretchedly poor. What there was of the corn, however, had been pronounced to be uncommonly good, and as such able to bear a greater amount of adulteration. But this soon turned out to have been a false idea ; and many a foolish improvident peasant who had rested upon it, as they will do upon any excuse against active exertion, found himself not only in want, but in want earlier than usual. The peasants of this part of the world make up their minds too passively to suffer every winter, as a necessary concomitant of the season, to take warning for any extreme occasion. They are accustomed, before the winter is far advanced, to mix their bread largely with less nourishing materials ; and before the winter is finally dismissed, to take the fodder from their stinted animals to feed themselves, and to unthatch their barns and dwellings to feed them. But this year all these extreme signs of scarcity showed themselves much sooner than is commonly the case, added to much illness among men and animals, attributable to want and unhealthiness of weather combined. How utter starvation did not occur would be a wonder to many ; but the Lettish peasantry, like the Scotch, help one another to the utmost of their power, and thus keep off positive destruction from some, by equalizing the misery among all.

The party at Sellenküll were tolerably prepared by Mart's industry to weather a hard season themselves, and also to help their neighbours through it ; and, though this was required to a much greater extent than had been expected, Mart both gave and lent cheerfully, and worked harder and fared harder than usual. His vexatious trials had not ceased. His enemy sought every opportunity to oppress and annoy him ; and it required all the young man's forbearance to fulfil his unjust tasks and keep his temper.

It is difficult, however, to ruin a sensible and an industrious man in any line of life, and Mart's unvarying steadiness seemed to bring even malice to a stand still. The season was arrived also when but little work can be done, or rather, need be done ; and when the many hours of darkness encourage a feeling of slothfulness which is an indulgence to the indolently disposed, and a relief to the scantily fed. Mart, however, had no pleasure in being idle ; as long as daylight lasted there was enough for him to do in repairing his house and farming buildings, and in attending to the wants of his domestic animals; and when darkness fell, he might be seen returning with a bundle of small split fresh wood in his hand—those candles of the northern peasantry —beneath the light of which, seated next the great stove, he plied many a domestic handicraft. This was the time when Anno got many a help in various household labours which another husband would have spurned as woman's work; but there was that about Mart which the meanest occupation could not degrade. He might have helped to bake the bread, or turn the wheel, and perhaps he sometimes did, and nobody could have called him unmanly.

Anno was indeed favoured among women. Not only were her own house duties diminished by a strong hand and eased by a sweet temper, but she was spared also all those other feudal burdens which fall upon the women of these provinces. The same ancient tenure which imposed three days' labour in the week upon Mart, required also from his wife certain days' spinning or carding during the winter for the benefit of the proprietor of the estate—usually performed at the mansion-house itself, but now, in its present untenanted condition, at that of the *Disponent*. Liso had fulfilled this as long as she had been able; and now it was naturally expected that the young assistant which Mart had taken into his service in the shape of a wife, and who had no family to require her attendance—not that this makes any difference—ought to take this duty on herself: but Mart thought differently; he paid another woman in the coin most acceptable— viz., in a small quantity of corn—to take her place, and Anno never entered the *Disponent's* doors.

This and the increasing want around them soon bore hard upon Mart's winter stock; it was obvious something must be done to replenish it, or he would himself need the help he was giving. Mart lost no time in considering whether he should eke out the remainder by denying it to his neighbours, or by adulterating it to themselves: he had no idea of feeding Anno upon straw, and so he asked for extra work at daily wages.

This was quite a novelty here. It was true that a landed proprietor occasionally returned from a tour or residence in some more civilized and better governed land with new systems of agricultural economy, and among the rest with that of labour for wages; but they left behind them the order and the justice necessary to preside over such matters, and the result only increased the peasant's natural hatred for innovations. Most of the ignorant peasantry could not understand the pro's and con's of such a question; a few saw that in a country so scattered in population no medium of payment could be so inconvenient as that of money; and all were perfectly aware that, what with needy masters and dishonest *Disponents*, they were likely to get little enough even of that.

Mart, however, was too clear-minded to be prejudiced, and too young to be cautious—though his late experience had taught him something he would gladly have unlearnt—and when the *Disponent* assented to his request, and allotted him some timber-felling at a certain rate of payment, he returned home with a sense of satisfaction which shone in every feature.

This extra labour was as much as he could get through with; he was hearty and robust, and it required no little solid nourishment to keep up the strength thus taxed. His father-in-law did not fail to tell him, with many a characteristic proverb, that it would answer his purpose just as well to sleep more and eat less; but Mart hated such maxims, and, even granting them true, he knew that work was good for man. His grandmother, too, occasionally put in a word of wisdom, and advised him to have no more dealings than necessary with a man who had shown all the will to injure him, and possessed all the power; but Mart, for once, differed from her, and said there was more to be gained by trust than by caution—and we will hope that he was right in the main.

Mart would have liked best to have received payment every week, but for that he had made no stipulation; he therefore laboured on till the job was just completed, and then, as his little cart was required to take wood to a neighbouring estate where corn was to be purchased, he went to Ian's house and asked for payment.

The *Disponent* counted over the work, and reckoned the days; it amounted in all to seventeen roubles—quite a fortune—but fairly earned. Mart stood by with his honest, open, beaming expression; the other sat at his desk with one which it was difficult to define.　Then he pulled out some old account-books, and seemed to be casting up sums, and Mart waited patiently, for he saw that he had other business on hand.　The man was indeed a villain; he knew that he was about to defraud the labourer of his hire, and he could deliberately cast up figures with a steady hand.　After a little while had elapsed he handed the young man a paper, on which he stood debtor for a number of days' work and half-days' work which, taken at a certain estimate, gave a total of sixteen roubles and a half; while on the other side he stood creditor for the labour just completed to the amount, as we have said, of seventeen roubles, thus leaving a difference of half a rouble.　This statement would have puzzled most; and as for Mart, he looked at it with the most utter guileless ignorance.　Then with an unblushing face and with impudent words, the *Disponent* explained that old scores must be paid before new ones; that it was time that the debts to the estate should be discharged; and that, in short, these were old liabilities of Mart's father which were now raked up, whether true or not, to defraud the son.

Mart was thunderstruck; his mind could not understand the villainous manœuvre; such a proceeding was unheard of even in this land of oppression, and he stood at first more amazed than indignant.　He then tried reason.　The *Disponent* referred him to the books.　He tried expostulation; and the *Disponent* bid him begone, for that he had not time to listen to the complaints of every idle fellow on the estate.　Then Mart tried—it went sore against his will, but he knew who depended upon him—he tried to move the brute; he told him that it was a hard year for the poor—that there was nothing but starvation around, and that he had others to maintain as well as himself.　And the *Disponent* replied with his demoniacal grin, that as long as he could afford to pay another woman to do his wife's work, he could want for nothing.

Then Mart flamed up, and a stream of hot indignation came boiling from his breast: his words were few, but they hit full at his oppressor.　Still he spoke as to a man—the wretch answered as to a dog, and dared to tell him—Mart!—that if he was insolent he would have him beaten!

Good heavens! how was honest and high spirited blood,

albeit only in the veins of a poor Livonian, to bear this, and flow on calmly after it. The bad man before him knew not what he had provoked. For the tempter was busy at that young and injured breast—putting bitter for sweet, and evil for good—bidding him fell the savage where he stood, and urging him to spring at that throat which had lied so foully to him. But the irritated man was not left to himself at a moment when all power over self was gone. An unseen arm interposed, and his was mercifully stayed. Mart flung the half-rouble, which he found, he knew not how, in his grasp, in the *Disponent's* face, and rushed out of an atmosphere which was suffocating him.

For a moment he felt that his neighbours had been right and he wrong ; for a moment he doubted whether God loved justice and hated iniquity ; but after he had been alone a few minutes the first fever of the turbulent spirit passed away, and, in a sudden return of right feeling, Mart lifted up his heart in thankfulness for having been brought out of that hateful house with innocent though defrauded hands.

Still a bitter and an angry feeling remained behind—one which, if wrong, it was much more difficult to think so—for the young and hopeful heart had been injured and insulted, and felt that henceforth it would be injured and insulted as often as might suit the malice or the interest of his implacable foe. His forbearance was of no use—his industry of no help—the future stretched itself out before him in one long vista of endurance, or ended in some dark deed of despair. He was obliged to continue his journey. It was well he had no companion—sympathy with a mind in this state only feeds the flame—resistance fans it.

> " Words weaker than his rage
> Would make rage more."

He unloaded his cart, and set his face towards his home. He had never before approached it with a heart so out of tune. He had never before dreaded to meet Anno's smile of trust or Liso's look of resignation, or felt that the one could bring bitterness to his heart and the other irritation to his temper.

As he plodded gloomily along, he came to a turn in the road which led to a great territorial mansion in the distance. It was the *Hakenrichter's*. Mart knew that the law protected the peasant from injustice and cruelty; but he knew also that, administered as it usually was, the law was only a dead letter, and that this man of all others was least likely to render it otherwise. There is a perverse pleasure, however, to an angry man in choosing to look at things as they should be, and not as they are. He turned up the road. His heart and steps were alike heavy, and, as he walked along with stooping shoulders and sunken head, it must be owned that he looked very much like any other Livonian peasant.

Poor Mart! he was too much engrossed in his own bitter reflections to know well what he was about; and, little dreaming that the *Hakenrichter* from within saw all who approached, he utterly forgot to observe a law of these modern Gesslers, which commands that no peasant should venture to approach or pass their mansions without uncovering their heads.

He went up to the back door, requested to speak to the *Erra* (or master), and was agreeably surprised by being at once admitted into that kind of stewy unventilated room in which *Erras* in this country delight. Whatever hopes might have been raised by his prompt admission, however, they were as instantly quenched. The gentleman was in that state of mind most approved in Russia for administering justice—in other words, he was in a towering passion; and, before Mart could make his best bow, broke forth thus:

" Are you the fellow who passed the house just now?—speak —hold your tongue—are you the fellow ?"

Mart admitted he was just come.

" And don't you know better, you rascal, than to strut past a nobleman's house with your filthy cap on, as if it were a *krug,* or one of your own pigsties?—pig that you are !"

Mart murmured that he had not seen the *Erra* or—

" Hold your tongue this moment, and speak the truth if you can. What matters it whether you see me or not? and what care I for such a fool as you ! You shall bow your vile head to my house, were I never to enter its doors from one year's end to another ! and you shall bow to my hat too, if I choose ;"—the *Hakenrichter* did not know how classical was the allusion—" or I 'll have your back broken. What do you say? Speak out !— hold your tongue ! Come to complain of the *Disponent !* I 'll cure you of complaining, you impudent rascal. Tell him to give you a sound beating like a dog as you are. Pig!—liar!—fool!—get out."

This was the substance of the speech, of which we have given a mitigated version—for it was plentifully garnished with various oaths and epithets, which would not translate into elegant English —delivered also with gestures which, as usual in such cases, portended a quick following up of blows.

Mart did not wait to be dismissed twice. He strode back through the *Volkstube,* or servants' apartment, at a rate which astounded its inmates, gained his little horse and cart, and, in order to avoid passing near the windows, struck into a side road which took him six wersts out of his way. The cup was full. He felt that the sullen, care-for-nothing desperation, which he had so often deprecated in his fellow-peasants, had now come home to himself. He threw himself into his cart, and lay there upon his face, like any other lazy boor. The road was execrably bad, full of great holes and stones; and many a jolt and fling did he get as the poor little tired animal dragged the unusual load painfully along.

At length the road divided into two. The animal chose the best, but it was the wrong one. Mart sprung up, dealt the horse a blow, and plucked the head furiously round. The poor dumb creature stood still with a meek, patient look. This broke the spell! How Mart hated himself! He leapt from the cart, his own generous self again, and passed his arm over the animal's neck, as he was often wont to do. The poor thing turned fondly to him; and master and beast walked on together, each with their load considerably lightened.

Mart's heart was now as soft as a child's. Nothing in that whole bitter day did he at this moment look back upon with such bitterness as upon his unprovoked treatment of his faithful beast. Anger and pride passed away, and love for his fellows and trust in his God returned; and, though he reached home that night with nothing to give and little to hope, yet his Anno's smile of trust was balm to his heart, and his grandmother's look of resignation strength to his soul.

CHAPTER VII.

THE question was now, how they were possibly to get through the many months that must still elapse before Nature would supply the help that man denied. The case looked desperate enough. But, as old Liso said, it was easy to praise God when the granary was full ; though even then they too often forgot to do so. When it was empty was the time to trust Him. Not but what she lamented the anxiety and labour that now devolved on her beloved grandson, and wished he could be relieved of two members of his family—herself and old Karria Pois—who were each of them, she said, of no use except to love him. But Mart chided her affectionately, and told her that love was more useful than anything else in the world : and we think so too.

The family at Sellenküll were not yet devoid of resources. There were stores of various kinds in the house and farm, which could be converted by a circuitous process into corn, and there were even a few roubles which Mart had husbanded up beside ; but the end of all these was easy to foresee, and then how was more to be obtained ! Mart had seen many a neighbour go down gradually in the world, never to lift up his head again, by the same process which was now hanging over him, and thoughts of despondency would occasionally arise ; but he braced up his heart manfully, felt that now was the time to fight and not to give way, and determined that, let Ruin knock ever so loudly at his gate, no act of his should let it in.

The fruits, too, of many a thrifty habit now appeared. Many an armful of fodder had Mart brought in, collected at times when nobody else worked, and from waste places which all neglected ; and for the support of his cattle there was no immediate fear. Mart held fast to the old Lettish proverb which says, " The cow gives milk by the mouth, and the hen lays eggs by the bill ;" and his well-fed animals verified it. In short, wherever he looked on his own domain, he found the result of always doing things well at the time, and this cheered him to do more.

Mart went to the pastor after service next Sunday, and told him the treatment he had received. But he did not attempt to seek for justice, nor did the pastor offer to obtain it ; for both knew that where an unjust *Hakenrichter* and a cruel *Disponent* coalesce against the peasants, their power of injury far outdoes his power of protection, and only increases with the least show of it.

The good old man was serious and low. The sight of his congregation told many a tale of woe. He had seen sullen men, and suffering women, and sharp-boned children among them, and felt that his interest in their spiritual welfare would have come home to their hearts with more effect if seconded with the relief of their bodily wants. Not that this occurred to his hearers. They were fallen to the worst symptom that can appear in a nation or in a community ; their only thought was how little they could live upon, and how long they could hold out. Relief from others seemed as visionary as help from themselves, and they listened with meek hearts to the address which exhorted them to patience and trust.

Not but what the pastor had done, and still did, his utmost to relieve them. He had drained his granary soon after harvest by supplying seed-corn to many a peasant too degraded and reduced to care for the consequences of leaving his ground unsown ; a small quantity was also distributed every week among the families most in need. Still it was nothing when subdivided among the numbers requiring it ; and, in truth, to have provided them with one week's sufficient maintenance would have been utterly beyond the good man's power.

He gave Mart, however, a job for the next week, at so much per day. " It is a pity such hands as yours should be idle, Mart ; and you may be sure of your money, although so little of it."

Mart thanked him with a happy face once more ; and, leaving the *Pastorat*, joined the congregation in the walk home to the village.

It was seldom he came in for any of the news and gossip of the little community, and it would have been better for his peace if he had not now ; for there was but one prevailing theme. Not the scarcity and unhealthiness of the season, for that was looked upon as too much God's doing to be murmured at, but the many and increasing cruelties of the base-born tyrant over them. There were stories which made Mart's very heart sick. Of boys who had been overworked, of girls who had been defrauded of their little earnings—of both who had been dreadfully beaten and misused. Then there were men lying at home ill with the effects of corporal punishment ; some for having neglected work or pilfered trifles ; but most for having merely turned like the worm when they were trodden upon.

Mart was wretched. Every word seemed to pluck at those bitter bad feelings which he hated more even than the wickedness which roused them. He left the groups, and dropped back to the *Brautwerber*, who was walking behind, his eyes, as usual, on the ground, and his puny little boy toiling along by his side. But this was not the way to change the current of Mart's thoughts. He knew, and so did everybody else, that Juhann's weakly looks and habitual depression were the result of one of those acts of intolerable tyranny of which so many had just been related. He had been beaten under semblance of the law, but in reality to gratify the malice of a master who always found law in Russia for all his cruelty ; and he had never held up his head after it. The man's spirit was broken !

Mart, as we have seen, could do more with him than anybody else, and generally managed to brighten up the moody though gentle face of his friend. But this time his heart failed him. In his good-humoured way he took hold of the child's other hand, and walked on for a minute or two in silence. Then suddenly he stopped, for Mart was towing away both father and child at an unconscionable rate ; and it struck him all at once that the little feet lingered.

" Are you tired, my little fellow ?"

" *Ja, vegga* "—yes, very—said the poor child. In a moment he was seated aloft on a firm arm, the little pale face close to Mart's still ruddy cheek.

"How light he is," said Mart inadvertently, as he pressed the squalid tiny form to him. A pang shot over the father's face.

"Yes," said he, "he is skin and bones, like all of us; chopped straw does not make man's flesh. The church-cart will have many a journey, but all light ones this year."

Mart pretended to laugh off this speech. "But your little boy has been very ill; no wonder he is so thin. It is well he got through that fever at all."

"Better still if he had not, perhaps; but Death does not take the offered child: but he'll go this winter, and the other too."

"It is wrong to say that," said Mart; and they walked on in silence till they reached Juhann's dwelling. It was not often that Mart had time to see into one of his neighbours' interiors; and none could offer a stronger contrast to his own than this. The *Brautwerber's* farm was one of the most miserable in the miserable village. The little barn and cowshed were quite unroofed, to feed those whom it no longer protected from the cold, and the house itself was not in much better condition. The roof had sunk; the posts had given way; and the doorway, wider and lower even than usual, seemed an entrance far more fitted for animals than for men, and was in truth quite as much used as such by the one as the other.

Mart bowed his lofty head, and went in. The first moving objects that became visible through the smoky atmosphere were three gaunt, high-backed pigs—one of which was busy with its snout grubbing in a low crib filled with filthy straw, which apparently constituted the only family bed. Farther on was a shapeless mass on the floor, which, but for two little skeleton legs which dangled from it, might have been taken for some unclean beast also. As the men entered, the legs agitated themselves rather violently. The mother, for she it was, now got up from the kind of lair, where, like an animal, she had been brooding over her young, and let a little thing of two years old drop from her. It stood for a moment tottering, then tumbled and roared. The father advanced, took it up tenderly, and hushed it: it was evident the children loved him, and he them, in spite of what he had said. But oh! what a home this was for a man to come to!

No Livonian will let a friend enter his door without setting something before him to eat, and bread was put upon the board. Such bread Mart had seldom seen : chaff was the principal ingredient, corn the least. The loaf was as light in proportion as the poor children it failed to nourish. And as Mart looked at the thin limbs and large bodies of the innocent little beings, he saw at once the result of a long continuation of such diet.

Juhann did not press his friend to do more than break the bread—a process too easily accomplished ; for it failed in all the properties of adhesion : but he gave a piece to the children, who swallowed it as quickly as it passed their lips, as if mastication were thrown away upon such materials.

" Is there nothing to drink ?" inquired the *Brautwerber* of his wife. " Where is the milk ?"

" The cow is dry, and the calf is dead ; but there is water," said the woman.

" Yes," said Juhann, " water enough." And, stealing a bitter smile at Mart, he added, " Water in the oven :" this being a Lettish phrase expressive of extreme dearth.

Wretched thoughts accompanied Mart in his lonely walk home, and some self-upbraidings too ; for, compared with this household, and too many he knew were like it, his was rioting in abundance. A good sound rye loaf, big as a log of wood, and something like it in appearance, with a little butt of milk, found their way to the *Brautwerber's* door before many hours had elapsed. Mart took to water from that evening.

But one bitter thought there was which would not be so easily banished. It had long glimmered dimly in his breast : and now that walk home from church fanned it up into feverish strength, making him start with terror from his sleep at night, and bringing a deep flush across his face by day. It was the thought lest that which had broken his poor friend's spirit and health should ever come home to him. The mere possibility seemed too great a degradation, and, situated as he was, the probability was too obvious. Anything else in the shape of personal endurance that his mind could conjure up he felt could be borne. He could bear being starved by inches, or worked to the bone ; he could stand foul language, and submit to wringing injustice. But to receive from the hands of another such ignominy as the most brutal master scarcely bestows on his most wretched beast ;

F

to deny that he had been born a man ; to forget that he was
to die one ; and to stand an animal in all save its dumbness, and
be *beaten!* this he felt was beyond his powers of endurance ;
and, if inflicted, would leave him either a villain or an idiot.
Fervently did he vow to himself to guard every word and deed
rather than give his enemy the slightest opportunity for that,
which every other indignity, if necessary, should be endured to
avoid.   And deliberately also had that enemy vowed to himself
to wait his time, and watch his opportunity, but that with nothing less should his vengeance be satisfied.

Meanwhile the job at the pastor's was completed, and Mart
was left to his own devices for obtaining corn.   These were not
few, and but too much time to put them into execution.   The
day was spent in tracking and snaring game—the game-laws
being a source of oppression which the Russian government still
holds in reserve.   A space was hewn clear by his strong arm in
the deep, frozen stream before their door, and kept so, where
many a primitive mode of attracting and catching the cold fish
beneath was adopted—once even a seal was caught,—and when a
little sledge-load of this kind had been collected—for it matters
not how long the frozen booty is kept—a journey was undertaken
to distant estates where resident families gave promise of a sale.
The reward of such journeys was very inadequate to the time
and labour, for sometimes man and horse toiled fifty or sixty
wersts, out and home, for a small sum, which the poverty of one
buyer, or the hackling meanness of another, cut down to the
lowest, without regard either to the labour that had earned or the
want that needed it.

It may be asked here, and naturally, why, with all these materials for food around them, the starving population did not avail
themselves of them in their natural state? why they did not
themselves consume the game in their woods and the fish in
their rivers?   But this is only one of the many instances of the
want of simple sense which exists in a half-civilized land.   They
look upon bread as the great necessary for man's sustenance, and
to whatever expedients they may resort to eke out a scanty or a
bad supply, they would starve rather than attempt to substitute
any thing else in its place.

Nor were Mart's expeditions without excessive hardship, and

even danger. His fine person was well defended with all that the care and industry of his young and his old wife, as he called them, could supply. The thick woollen stockings, the coarse fingerless gloves, were always mended or renewed,—the brown woollen coat had never a button missing,—the cover-all sheep-skin never a hole unstopped,—and as Anno helped to equip her kind and manly helpmate for these expeditions, and he first bent down his tall head, while she pulled out the curls which her wrappers had confined, and then raised it again with one of his beaming smiles, Anno thought in her innocence that not even the *Ghossudar* himself could carry a sweeter face upon his shoulders! Certainly, since ignorance was bliss, it had been especially folly in this case to be wise; for poetical delusions are too few among this suffering race for any of them to be wantonly destroyed, and an abstract faith in the perfection of his present Majesty is certainly one of the most poetical. Personal beauty she might have found on the Imperial countenance more than she could appreciate, but as for the heart that shines through, God help poor Anno, and all his subjects!

To return, however, to a better man. The second month in the year was now advanced—snow lay in unusual quantities, and an intense frost had set in. The country was open to whoever liked to take the shortest way across it, and Mart and his faithful little horse toiled over many a swamp which in summer never felt the foot of man, and rarely even in winter. Karria Pois he always left at home, where he was more wanted than trotting by his master's side. Sometimes Mart's sledge was the first to force a toilsome track where none had passed before; often the first to resume one which the last few days of snow had covered over.

This was all very well in fine, still weather, though even then the exposure was cruelly severe; but in journeys of this length he who started in sunshine might return in snow-drift, when the signs on earth and sky were both hidden to the traveller, and man and horse, after floundering bewildered along, might either find themselves thrown out of all knowledge of the road, or returned to the same spot they had left hours before. Many, in like case, have stopped never to go on again, and Mart needed all his energy to resist the benumbing effects from without and

within.   For the spare diet to which he had been reduced for
many weeks told especially at a time when he needed the best;
and the bitter blast chilled his warm, young blood as it had never
done before.   There in a desolate, pitiless wild, with a black,
porous, blotting-paper looking sky above him, and the thick,
falling snow fast obliterating every means of guidance that still
remained around, the weary man often halted with a failing heart,
and, unseen but by One, looked to but One for succour.   Then
the arm was passed fondly over his horse's neck—the willing
creature started again with fresh courage—for the Livonian
peasant horse, like his master, only requires good usage to make
him the most valuable servant, and often his instinct alone took
them right home.

From the two women, who waited anxiously for the benighted
traveller, Mart kept many an adventure of this kind, or made
light of it; but the weariness of his frame, equally as the hours
of intense dead slumber which renovated it, told what he concealed.   Mart's home was worth returning to: there was not
only comfort and union, but there was the crown of them both
—refinement.   If Anno had ever known the grossnesses of life
incidental to misery and hardship, the atmosphere of care and
protection in which she had lived since her marriage had completely removed them from her mind; she had cast them off as
a sound limb does unsound flesh.   While old Liso took higher
ground: misery, and the coarsest misery, too, she had known
plenty of, but her mind was raised above it.

Nothing gives so high a tone to a family circle in any rank of
life as the influence of an aged woman who possesses the double
wisdom both to edify and to attract.   We say an aged woman,
because there is something in old age itself which partakes more
of the feminine than of the masculine character; not only on account of its weakness, but in the strength which, as with the
female sex, at every age, they have through that very weakness.
Also there is something in the wisdom of a really experienced
female mind which seems to us more applicable to the general
needs of human nature than in that of her fellow man; partly
perhaps from being drawn from sources which, occupying an
apparently subordinate position in the affairs of this life, vary
less with their changes, but chiefly in being more really and

closely connected with the vital principles of the Christian religion.

There was much in old Liso's character and manner which might be compared to those admirable aged women of God not unfrequently found in the Scotch Presbyterian Church. Like them she had all that intelligence and refined mode of expression in the midst of poverty and hardship, which, however wonderful it may seem, is easily to be accounted for; for who can retain commonplace ideas or vulgar speech who know the Bible by heart, as Liso did, and as those to whom we have compared her generally do.

Besides all this, the good old grandmother had a sweet countenance, which goes for much in a person's merit and attractiveness—and rightly—since whatever may be said of the gift of beauty, every one makes the best part of their own face.

To both wife and grandmother, in spite of Mart's prudence and discretion, these journeys became a source of anxiety. Anno suggested the plan of greater economy of the stock in hand, rather than of further such laborious efforts to replenish it. Her father, she said, always mixed the corn with straw, even in the best years; and, in bad ones, for aught she knew, it was made of nothing else. And Mart answered, that certainly she had thriven wonderfully well on such diet, but that still he could not afford to rob his cattle to feed her.

"No, Anno," he said, "I may have hard nights and days too, sometimes, out in this weather, but I should have harder still to sit at home and see you eat bad bread, and know that others had none at all." And this silenced Anno.

Liso had other anxieties; she felt that this mode of existence was worse even for mind than for body. She knew that there were charms for the young in a free, uncontrolled life, however hard; that there were snares for the generous and credulous in the strange and wild company he necessarily fell in with, and that there was sore temptation for the cold and weary in many an isolated *Krug*, or public-house; which, in Livonia, bear no better character with sober old grandmothers than they do anywhere else. But Liso stuck fast to the old Lettish motto, and a beautiful one it is—"*Work and pray.*" The first, her growing infirmities considerably hindered in her own estimation; but the second, in her own language, thanks be to God, she neither wanted eyes, nor ears, nor hands, nor feet for. "Better," she said, with another proverb, "a prayer behind the door than a scolding before the stove;" and some parents would not be the worse of thinking so too.

CHAPTER VIII.

As we have said before, Mart kept most of his lost ways an overturns in drifts and such incidents from the two women; bu one incident he could not conceal. The scarcity and hardness o₁ the season affected the inhabitants of the forest as well as those of the villages, and the wolves came out from their fastnesses, with a boldness they do not often show. Many a single one and even couples together had skulked across Mart's path with an evil look, but quickened their retreat at that shrill shout, at the top of his voice, which he had practised since a child.

One evening his way home led through a desolate morassy wood, which stretched for ten wersts on one side of his little farm, and where the track, deep between accumulations of high snow, gave only just sufficient width for the little horse and sledge. Mart's eyes were closed and his senses heavy with weariness, nevertheless he soon began to be aware that the animal was quickening its pace unwontedly; again it jerked forward— quicker still—and a low neighing sound of terror effectually roused the drowsy man. He looked in front; all was as usual—a wild scanty forest, standing knee-deep in a bed of snow—the narrow trough of a track winding through it—here and there pyramids of snow which showed the huge ant-hills of the country —the heavens bright—the earth white—not a living object but the horse before him. He looked behind—the scene was just the same—white snow, and leafless trees, and a winding track; but close to the sledge were three dark gaunt animals, heavily gallop- ing, and another was fast gaining behind. The jaws of the fore- most, with the lowness of the sledge, were within reach of Mart's shoulder. He cared not for that—he knew that it was his horse they wanted *first*; and saw in an instant that all depended on the animal's courage more than on his own. If the frightened creature

could have the nerve to keep steady in the track, the chances
were much in its favour, for the moment the wolves turned off
in order to pass and get ahead of it, the depth of the snow diminished their speed ; but should the horse, in its terror, plunge
aside and flounder in the snow, Mart knew that it would be lost.
He leaned forward, called the animal cheerfully by its name,
and laid his hand on its back as he was often wont to do, in times
of fatigue or difficulty—the poor beast knew the kind voice and
hand—raised its ears, which were laid flat back with terror, and
fell into an evener pace.

Mart shouted violently—but the wolves were either too keen
or too many—it made no impression.   It was an awful time both
for master and horse.   Mart kept his hand on the animal, while
his eye watched the ferocious brutes, who were often within
arm's length.   He had a hatchet, which he always carried on
these occasions, to chop the frozen fish ; he felt for it and grasped
it in his hand, but forbore to use it, for the closer the wolves
kept at the back of the sledge, the less were they seen by the
horse.   Every minute, however, one or more of them broke out
of the track in the attempt to pass ; and although they instantly
lost footing in the snow, yet the unblinkered eyes of the little
animal had caught sight of the dreaded foe, and a plunge forward
made Mart turn his eye with anxiety to see that it kept straight
in the narrow track.

One of the wolves was more than usually huge and long-
limbed, and more than once it had contrived, in spite of the deep
snow, to advance nearer abreast of the sledge than any of its
companions.   Upon this grim creature Mart more especially
kept watch, and caught the green light which played from its
eyeballs.   It turned off again—the snow laid fleeter for a space
—the wolf kept its footing—it gained—for their pace is enormous
—the little horse's eye glared round at it.   Mart withdrew his
hand, wet with the animal's perspiration ; the wolf was just
beyond arm's reach, but he kept his hatchet in readiness.   The
horse was now in desperate gallop, and the wolf just abreast—it
suddenly turned sharp towards it—now was Mart's time.   He
dealt a tremendous blow—the wolf avoided it, but stumbled in
the snow, and in a moment was yards behind.

The distance from home was now quickly shortening beneath

the horse's hoofs, which continued to carry the sledge at full gallop, till the fear of an overturn became a source of fresh anxiety.   Mart was quite aware by this time that these were no common lazy wolves he had to deal with, but sharp-set determined brutes, to whom man or beast would be alike welcome. These were not the animals to be deterred by the signs of man's dwelling, as is usually the case, and there was an ugly werst of wide open space between the outskirts of the forest and his house, which he looked to with real apprehension.

They were now at the very edge of the wood—the road became opener—the wolves gained on each side—the horse bounded furiously forward, caught the sledge against the stump of a tree —it overturned—was swept away at a tremendous pace, and Mart was left alone in the snow.   In a moment a heavy claw had slit the throat and down the front of his sheepskin—it was well Anno's wrappers lay so thick beneath.   He threw off the brute and rose—his hatchet had been jerked out of his hand in the fall —he cast a desperate glance around, but saw it not.   The horse was now almost out of sight, two of the wolves were close to the defenceless man, and the two others, deserting the animal, were bounding back to him.   Mart faced the foremost, he could do no more, and in an instant was surrounded.

Here we must leave him, however cruel it may seem.   Meanwhile the two women were as usual expecting him anxiously at home—for Mart was late.   Anno was sitting beneath the pine-wood candle at the spinning-wheel.   Liso had risen from her's and gone into the smaller chamber, especially devoted to her. Old Karria Pois was lying before the stove fast asleep.   Of a sudden the dog pricked up his ears, listened, rose—ran to the door and whined—then, returning to Anno, wagged his tail, ran back and whining again, scratched at the door.   Karria Pois usually gave signal of Mart's approach, though not in so urgent a way, and Anno opened the door expecting to see her husband. The dog dashed furiously out, but no sign of Mart appeared. The young wife went out into the piercing air—saw and heard nothing, and was slowly turning in, when a sound caught her ear —it was the sound of hoofs striking full and sharp upon the frozen ground.   So had Mart never approached before.   But there was no time for wonder, for the next moment the horse galloped up to the door and stopped. Anno saw instantly that something had happened—the animal was dripping with foam and trembling all over—the sledge was reversed, and, above all, Mart was not there.

Anno was but the girl still; she called quick to her grandmother—the old woman did not answer—she flew into the inner room; Liso was standing motionless with her face turned from the door. There was no light, save from the little snowed-up window; but Anno saw enough to know that she stood in prayer. "Oh! *Jummal!*" (God) said the poor girl to herself, "hear her!" and leaving her undisturbed, she ran again out of the house, gave one look at the trembling horse, and then all trembling herself, began to retrace the jagged track in which it had come.

We must now return to Mart, whom we have left in a frightful position. He knew what it was to put forth his strength in games and wrestling-matches, and it was such as, shoulder to shoulder and muscle to muscle, few could withstand. But it was as nothing now against the heavy weight—the vice-like teeth—the rending grasp that held him down on every side. For a few seconds the desperate violence of a man to whom life is sweet, and such a death most horrible, shook off the pitiless assailants; but his own blood had dyed the snow, and the sight of it seemed to turn ferocity into fury. The blood-hounds closed again upon him—they pulled him down!

People say there is no time to think in sudden dangers:—they have never known one. There are more thoughts struck from the mind in one moment's collision with sudden and desperate peril than in days of fearless security. The sweets of this earth—the home that lay so near—the mystery of Heaven, swept over poor Mart's mind; nay, even particulars found time to intrude. He thought how Anno and Liso would watch through the night —how his mangled remains would tell all in the morning— Anno's despair—the village lament: he thought of all this, and more, and knew himself in the jaws of hungry wolves! Then those foul lurid eyes glared over him; the tightening of the throat followed, and thinking was over. Still he struggled to release his arms—the grasp on the throat was suffocating him— his senses reeled—when on a sudden—dash came another animal hard-breathing along; threw itself into the midst with one sharp howl, and fastened upon the chief assailant. The wolves relaxed their fury for an instant; Mart reeled giddily to his feet, and recognised his brave dog. For a second he stood stunned and bewildered; when he saw one wolf retreating, and all three attacking the dauntless Karria Pois. He turned to help him, and a bright object caught his eye; it was his hatchet lying on the snow within arm's length of his last struggle. Mart snatched it up, and was now himself again. Blood was dripping from him, but his limbs were uninjured, and furious were the strokes he dealt.

One wolf soon lay dead at his feet; the other cowed, and retreated, spilling its blood as it went, and held off, skulking round; and now Mart poured his whole fury on the great monster, which held Karria Pois in as stifling a grasp as he had done his master. It was no easy task to release the dog. The hatchet rung on the wolf's skull, rattled on his ribs, and laid bare the gaunt backbone; but the dog's own body interrupted any mortal wound, and the wolf seemed to feel no other. Poor Karria Pois's case was desperate; his legs were all drawn together, protecting the very parts he sought to wound, when suddenly he stretched himself out with some fresh agony, and the hatchet was buried deep in the wolf's throat. Many more fierce strokes were needed before life was extinct; and as Mart rose, a hand on his shoulder startled him, and his wife fell on his bosom.

"Mart!"

"Anno!"

Long did the young couple stand in speechless embrace; but the weaker supported the stronger, for Mart's manly nerve was gone, and he leant on Anno like a strengthless child.

"Mart, Mart! Oh! you are safe—dear Mart!" For all answer, Mart pressed her closer.

"But what is here?" for her hand which laid on his shoulder was wet with a warm clammy substance, and there was light enough to see that dark stain which nothing else is like.

"Mart! you are hurt—you are bleeding!" and going back a step, she saw for the first time her husband's condition. The two dead wolves—the gasping dog—the bloody and furrowed snow! and the full and dreadful truth came upon her and she burst into passionate sobs.

In truth Mart presented a frightful aspect; his sheepskin hung in strips, for each claw had cut it like a knife; his shoulder was bare, not only to the flesh, but to the bone; his long hair was dishevelled; every article of clothing was torn and awry. It was too evident that some dreadful struggle had taken place, and Anno now saw with *what.*

It was now Mart's turn to support; his strength was returned, and with it his unflagging sweetness.

"Anno! *Einohenne!* Anno! *pai!* don't cry so; I am safe and well, only a few scratches on my skin: you'll have to patch me up as well as my clothes. Let's attend to poor Karria Pois—nobody but you could have made me forget him—I fear he is more hurt than his master."

And the young couple leant over him and tenderly examined his wounds. Then with many tears Anno related how in the deepest sleep the faithful old dog had seemed to receive tidings of his master's danger; and Mart described how he had reached his side when his need was at the greatest—though he did not say how great that need had been—but Anno knew; and then both caressed him more and more.

There was life in the old dog yet, and more than they had ventured at first to expect; his throat was lacerated, his ear torn through, and many a bite and a rent had he on his body, but he licked the hands that felt his wounds, and, rising on his feet, shook a shower of blood from him. Then he deliberately smelt first at one wolf's carcass and then at the other, to ascertain that all was right, and having done this, hobbled off towards home as if he felt he was no further required.

"Come home, Mart; can you walk?" said Anno.

"Yes, yes, as well as ever; but I have not done with these grey men yet (this being a common appellation for the wolves by the peasantry); the night's work is worth two silver roubles to me; the rest of the brutes will be down their companions' throats before the morning;" and so saying he cut off the ears, by which token the Lettish peasant is entitled to a reward in money on showing it to a magistrate.

Mart was soon seated in his own warm house, waited on by his two tender companions, who examined his wounds and injuries with alternate horror and gratitude.

"You were praying for me, grandmother, Anno tells me, when she left the house ;— God heard you.   Never say again that you and old Karria Pois are of no use ; you two have saved my life."

These words were more than the venerable parent could bear with composure ; and she turned away to lift up her heart again.

"All have been of use to-night," said Anno in a low tone ; "grandmother, Karria Pois, even the poor horse ; only I have done nothing."

"You are my own *Einokenne*," said Mart, lower still, and leant his weary head against her.

"Now, Anno, *pai !* go and wash Karria Pois too."   This was done, and soon master and dog were deep in slumber.

CHAPTER IX.

THIS encounter put an end to Mart's journeys for the present;
not but what he speedily recovered from it, but it proved the
prelude to further aggressions from the same animal, though not
of so perilous a kind.   The wolf does not often attack man, except when flung helplessly before him, as Mart had been.   It is
the tenants of the farmyard, and not of the farmhouse, they seek.
Scarcely a night now elapsed without a calf, foal, sheep, or even
some poor famished cow or horse falling a victim—the dilapidated state of the buildings, which housed the miserable animals,
affording but too easy an entry.   In vain did Mart urge the
expenditure of a little hearty labour to make fast those which
remained.

"What will you do," he said to the *Brautwerber*, "in the
summer, when you want your calf to sell, and your colt to work?"

Juhann shook his head.

"The summer will never come for me," he said; and then
looked down at his attenuated hands and arms, which seemed
little able to wield an axe.   Mart mended his cow-shed for him
and for others besides.

But he was not satisfied with merely keeping the enemy out.
Accompanied by a few of the hardiest and least superstitious of
the peasants, and furnished with dogs and weapons, Mart headed
several expeditions in search of the ravenous animals, tracking
them by footmarks left but a few hours before, or by the fresh
blood-drops of some recent prey which accompanied them.

We mention the least superstitious of the peasants as most
disposed to follow Mart, because with many it is a rooted belief
that the destruction of one wolf only increases the rancour of his

companions. In cases where the traveller is hard pressed to escape from a pack of them, there is no doubt that the fall of one wolf, and the consequent taste of his blood, increases tenfold the voracity of the rest : but when the farmyard suffers from nightly invasion, it stands to reason that there is no help but to attack the invader.

Mart, however, met with much opposition in the matter ; his companions lagged away, or came unwillingly, and very few besides himself and the dogs thoroughly entered into the spirit of the chace. As for the dogs, they seemed to consider it as a happy opportunity for paying off many an old score, and it was difficult to call them back from a pursuit which, when once separated from their companions, could only lead to their destruction. Between dog and wolf there exists a natural hatred, which the one exhibits in an open tear-throat animosity, and the other in a relentless cunning. The wolf feigns flight to lead his victim on ; he imitates the whine of a dog to deceive him, and when the stratagems have led the courageous animal beyond protection, his doom is sealed.

Two or three fine young dogs thus fell a sacrifice to their rashness and inexperience, but Mart suffered no anxiety for Karria Pois ; he was the first to show his disapproval of any unnecessary valour, and to give the example of readiness in the retreat, as much as of courage in the onset : otherwise the expeditions were generally successful ; one or more pair of ears, or, if a young wolf, the skin, being the usual trophies they returned with ; and then Mart had regularly to incur a long journey in order to claim the reward adjudged by law : for the *Haken-richter* we have described was not likely to have any more of his visits, and the other nearest magistrate lived twenty-four wersts off.

By these and other means did Mart persevere in maintaining his own household, and helping many another. But it was heart-breaking work as the spring slowly advanced ; for, to the hardship of bad and insufficient nourishment were now added the effects of it, and coffin after coffin found its way to the dead-house in the churchyard, there to await the softening of the earth that was to receive it. The child not yet firm on its feet, the aged tottering on theirs, went first, and light were the coffins, as the poor *Brautwerber* had said they would be.

Old Tonno was the first to bring death into Mart's doors. The charge of him and his few remaining stock had been added to Mart's other cares, and indeed ever since the marriage of his daughter both Mart and Anno had contributed the work of their hands to supply his need and comfort. One Sunday he was missing from his seat in church, and that same afternoon Anno and Mart found the old man drooping at home, and, each walking by the sledge, brought him tenderly under their own roof.

There is something infinitely more touching, in some senses, in the death of the lowest beggar, than in that of the highest potentate upon earth. The little they have to renounce speaks so bitterly of the little they have enjoyed. There may be a sad moral to the human heart in their love of life, but there is a keen reproach in their indifference to it. Tonno had never had any philosophy, and not much religion, as far as was apparent. He had been a complainer all his life, very obstinate and rather sullen; but from the moment the hand of death was upon him he showed himself gentle, cheerful, and communicative, bestowed words of tenderness upon his daughter, and wholesome manly advice upon Mart. It had been remarked of him by many of his companions and contemporaries on the few occasions of festivity which had enlivened poor Tonno's life, that he always came out in very different colours from those he usually exhibited. Whether this was attributable to the warming influence of the liquids usually circulated on such occasions, mattered not; if this was intoxication, nobody wished to see him sober, for Tonno was never so likeable under any other aspect. It seemed always as if he wanted to forget his cares, to be himself.

But a deeper reason, though one we can little understand, lay beneath; for the approach of death had the same effect. It appeared as if he had thrown off a weight, or knew himself so near the time for doing so, that he no longer felt the burthen. He had not a regret for the past, nor an apprehension for the future. The pastor came and prayed with him. Tonno assented to all, especially to the sorrows and trials of this life, and the infinitely superior nature of that which was to come; but for faith of a higher sort there seemed no room in the old man's mysterious mind. There was nothing for it to do; no doubts to overcome; no regrets to subdue.

The pastor was accustomed to see odd exhibitions of the human character, among a race of people whose lives veer between the elevation of a saint and the grossness of an animal. A clergyman from a different country might have been puzzled or dismayed, but the good old man's fervid faith supplied that comfort which his poor simple sheep often denied him. He knew their hardships, and trials, and long-sufferings; he knew them to be inert and foolish, and mistrustful and suspicious of men, but he rarely knew them grasping, vindictive, or perfidious, and never questioning God's providence or doubting his word. He looked, therefore, at Tonno's sinking eye with mixed feelings; but love and faith were uppermost. As he left he expressed a hope, as most kind-hearted people do, that he might find him better on his next visit. "No! *Herr Pastor*," the dying man replied, "God seems to think that I have toiled and starved long enough: and so do I. So *Jummal aga*"—God be with you; and these were his last words.

To our usual standard of reasoning his death was not edifying, for the sources of that cheerfulness with which he welcomed it were incomprehensible, but it was unfeignedly touching.

Anno wept for him as a daughter, and Mart regretted him with a sincerity which a few days before he could not have thought possible.

The next call upon Mart's sympathies was from his poor friend. Mart's generous help had kept the family from starvation, but the seeds of death had long been sown. The Sunday after Tonno's funeral Mart carried a small light coffin to church. It was Juhann's youngest child; and the Sunday after that he assisted to lift a larger and heavier burden into the cart. It was his wife. Mart saw her placed by the side of her child in the mournful dead-house, and as he looked at them, and then round at the numbers it already contained, he did not pity them.

Then he came back and went in to comfort his friend.

Juhann and the child were seated side by side, in perfect silence, upon a bench before the stove, and, to all appearance, had sat there for hours. The little, pale, puny boy was always a touching object, and now, in this atmosphere of woe, more so than ever. The father's gloom seemed to have overshadowed it till it no longer loved the sun. It had no childish smiles nor ways : it was always patient and quiet, and looked as if it would never grow in body nor alter in mind.

It is difficult to address a silent mourner. Mart sat down next his friend and took the child on his knee. He said all he could, but extracted only monosyllabic answers, or none at all. At length, after a pause, he broke out : " This little fellow will be a burden to you now ; you had better let me take him home,— he will be well cared for." Then Juhann answered quick, " No, Mart, no ! Whenever I go, nobody but you and your wife shall have him, but we 'll live together as long as we can." So saying, he took the boy off Mart's knee and seated him again, meek and quiet at his side, and Mart left the pair with a heavy heart.

Every fresh sight of Juhann only renewed those feelings of pity for him and of dread for himself, which Mart with difficulty kept under. This thought was the besetting thorn in his path. He looked at it until he could not bear it ; he tried to banish it, and found it too deeply rooted. It hung over him like some evil prophecy. He felt that the very determination to avoid ignominy was making him fit for it. No violent word, no unjust task, now provoked a common share of indignation from Mart. The dread of that one possible dishonour seemed to extinguish a better feeling than itself. Mart was dissatisfied and out of tune ; it was the first poison in his life, for it undermined his self-respect.

If we have not mentioned the *Disponent*, it is not because he had at all abated in his rancorous persecution. Not one word, look, or action of Mart's had been overlooked ; he only bided his time.

Mart's independence and generous help to others all through the hard winter had been gall and bitterness to Ian's bad heart, and he now felt the effects in being suddenly required to work four days in the week at a large distillery recently erected on the estate. At another time the young man would have complained, or remonstrated—for this was an unjust imposition of labour—

but he had learnt wisdom, or rather, what he hated, cunning, and, hoping that a few weeks' work and patience would release him, he submitted without a word.

But this employment brought him into frequent contact with his enemy, and the perpetual chafe upon his temper was too much. Mart was not one of those pieces of perfection which look down serenely on trials they do not feel. No! he was generous and quick, and could not have been the one without the other. He was irritated, wanted to be angry, and dared not ; and the feelings became bitter and peevish, held in, which would have been manly and noble let out. For anger is a true thing, and it is not because it is wrong in us, but because it is too good for them, that we repress it either to the rogue or the fool, and then a worse feeling takes its place.

Mart grew gloomy. He could not be cross to Anno : she was too dependent on him ; but more than once was his head bowed into his grandmother's lap in sorrow for a hasty word, which he repented the more for knowing it to be so instantly forgiven.

" Oh ! grandmother," he said, " if I lose hope, I shall go down as many a better man has done before me. And I am losing it already."

But worse was to come for poor Mart, and a heavy day it was, when the *Disponent* informed him that he must move in a month into old Tonno's forsaken tenement ; for that he wanted to put somebody else into his. Mart bore this on his heart for two days, for he had learned to brood ; but then the mist before his better nature gave way, and he unburdened his heart to Anno and Liso, and comforted them by allowing them to comfort him.

Mart knew that the change was illegal—that no little hereditary tenant could be moved without full consent or full compensation ; but to whom could he complain ? The pastor he had forborne to trouble with his cares, for the old man's spirits were failing with the misery around him. But he went to him now, and simply told his tale. The pastor looked up into Mart's open face, and sighed as he saw how much care and want had sharpened it in the last three months.

" Don 't despair, Mart," he said ; " I have been young and

G 2

now am old ; yet never saw I the righteous forsaken.   God has
tried you, but he has also blessed you much this sad winter.   I
know how you have helped your neighbours.   Take my word, you
won't be forsaken ; only keep up a trusting and a patient heart.
I would say the same, could I help you as I wish I could ; for
Mart, believe me, it is as sore a trial for me to see all this going
on, and not be able to prevent it, as it can be to you to leave your
father's house ;" and the tears started into the old man's eyes.

"If the young baron were but here, I could do much, for I
know he has a kind and humane heart," said the old man, thinking aloud ; "such a good face too."

Mart asked when he was expected to return.

"Ah ! Mart, that I don't know.   He likes foreign countries
better than poor Livonia, and I don't much wonder at it," he
added with a heavy sigh.   The old man was low and sorrowful.
Mart thanked him, but determined in his heart not to burthen
him again with cares he could not mitigate.   Still he felt relieved, and, what he most needed, raised in his own esteem.
The pastor has spoken of him with respect and praise, and he
went home in a glow of better feelings.

Poor fellow ! they were doomed to be sadly tried.   Old Liso
was ill !   The aged frame had at length given way.   She had
borne much, and only a little more was needed to make that too
much.   The prospect of leaving the house she had so long
known supplied this.   She had not complained, and no one would
have guessed that the blow had struck so hard ; nor had it ; but
it was sufficient to upset what had been long tottering.

Our readers will have been surprised that no medical man
should have been summoned in these various emergencies, but
the nearest was sixty wersts off, and, had he been but six, the
maladies of the distressed village were such as no mere medical
advice could have much assisted.   Wholesome laws and just ad-
ministrators of them, and a kind and resident proprietor, were
the medicine they needed.   For old Liso, however, nothing
could now have helped.   She was past seventy years of age, and
among the poor Livonian peasants the term beyond which all
is vanity and vexation of spirit commences much earlier.

All night her grandchildren watched, and as the rising sun

threw its cold beams full through Liso's little dusky pane, Mart leaned over the humble bed and saw that the look of life was fast departing. The young peasant was alone with her whom he loved with a less absorbing, though more rooted, feeling than his wife, for he had never known the time when that feeling was not. The love for Anno had made him know himself to be a man, that for his grandmother had continued to keep him the child; and as he stood looking at the dear familiar face which had never had for him but that one look of which we never tire, sweet memories and gloomy forebodings rose together in his mind, and he groaned aloud.

Liso's failing senses responded to the sound. She stretched forth both her withered hands to him.

"Mart! my son! my son!"

Mart fairly gave way. "Oh! grandmother, grandmother! how shall I live without you? You are leaving me, when I need you most. I am sore encompassed."

Liso raised herself up. "My son! listen to me. If God were ever with me in this life, and He has never failed—He is now. He knows how heavy your cares and trials have laid at my heart, and now that I am leaving you encompassed with them, He gives me a peace I never knew before. Oh! such peace!" and Liso paused for breath. "God cannot lie. I am a poor wretched old creature, but He cannot deceive me—He is not waiting till I am gone to turn His back upon you. No, Mart; fear not! He will come to your help in His good time. Man's extremity is God's opportunity. I speak His thoughts—my own are gone."

Liso said all this in broken sentences. Still Mart held her hands in an agony of grief.

"Grandmother; I am weak and sinful. Man is hard upon me—very hard; and if God should hide his face, only for a little season, I fear to fall."

Liso withdrew her hands. With her last strength she folded them together, and repeated in a firm voice this verse from Isaiah,—"And though the Lord give you the bread of adversity, and the water of affliction, yet shall not thy teachers be removed into a corner. But thine eyes shall see thy teachers, and thine ears shall hear a word behind thee, saying, ' This is the way— walk ye in it—when ye turn to the right hand and when ye turn to the left.' "

So died the good old Liso, and her death was edifying, for the simplest heart could understand what it was that blunted its sting !

CHAPTER X.

THE young people were now left alone, to feel how much that pious old woman had been interwoven in every source of their happiness, even in those which each believed they derived exclusively from the other. Her loss, instead of drawing them closer together, seemed for a while to interpose a strangeness which neither could quite have accounted for. But the truth was, that Liso's age and experience, instead of making Anno appear younger and more ignorant, had had the contrary effect. The gentle time-worn matron and the timid inexperienced girl had blended so harmoniously together, that no one knew, till one was taken away, where their characters met, or where they divided. Then Mart found that he was left alone with one who depended upon him more than he had known, and Anno felt that she stood unassisted with a husband who was accustomed to more than she had given. But the blank, though painful, was right, for Liso deserved to be most missed in that which she had least displayed—in the importance she had given to Anno, and in the influence she had exercised over Mart. Her death too happened at a time when this would be most felt; for Mart, occupied with internal struggles, which none but his venerable parent could have shared, was less open than usual, and Anno, from that reason, thrown more on herself, was more timid.

The death of Liso and the changes in Mart's occupation had occasioned a kind of interregnum in which he had become comparatively unconscious of the sufferings of his poor neighbours; and meanwhile those sufferings had become greater than ever. The reader will weary of the monotony of our tale; but we tell it as it happened, and must happen in a country where man's laws help to make Nature's more unkind. The only variety in a seven months' winter which begins in scarcity, is that it sets in famine. This was the case now. The progress of the season told the truth only plainer. Long and light days were come, and men could no longer burrow in their smoky dens and sleep like animals; but came abroad with pallid cheeks and sunken limbs, and looked each other in the face. Strong men had become nervous and weak. Boys and girls looked sharp and old— young babes gave no pleasure to their mothers—aged parents were a burthen to their children. There was much brutal selfishness to make you weep for poor human nature, but also some traits of touching devotion—and where are these wholly absent?—to redeem it. The orphan was taken in—the church beggar was fed—some were helped who had no claim, and others were helped who could make no return.

The spring was unusually protracted. It was the beginning of May before the mountains of snow began to diminish and the rivers to unlock ; and it would be yet a full month or six weeks before vegetation would cover the earth, and relieve the starving peasant of the burthen of his starving cattle. This is especially the season which the poor of these countries can seldom, under any circumstances, weather without help—when the best managed supplies begin to fail both for man and beast. The peasantry bear long— too long! for woe befall a country whose inhabitants learn to abstain from necessaries—and now a cry arose from among them that the *Bauer Klete*, or peasants' granary, to which each is compelled to contribute, should at length be opened to them. For what had its contents been wrung from them, if they were not to be restored again in such an extremity? More than once, however, had a petition to this effect been made during the winter, but stoutly refused by the *Disponent*, who held the keys— backed, of course, by the *Hakenrichter*. The stores had not been opened for years; not, indeed, since the present *Disponent* had come into office.

On the following Sunday, therefore, a consultation was held among the chief peasants, after church, to consider the matter ; and it was determined that a deputation should wait upon the *Hakenrichter* to urge the petition—ostensibly because he was highest in authority, but really because most of them feared to approach the other bad man, under whom the whole village groaned and travailed in misery. The pastor also approved of this plan. He himself, unknown to the peasants, had endeavoured to negotiate for a supply, but received an answer which warned him, for their sakes, not to appear on the present occasion. Also, he felt that the petitioners carried that misery on their very persons, which no further evidence was required to confirm. It was plain that if the resources of the *Bauer Klete* were intended to relieve those who had the double claim both of needing them and having supplied them, that time was now more than come. Mart was requested to join, but refused, and returned home.

The deputation set out immediately. They found the *Hakenrichter*, and obtained from him a written order for the doors of the *Bauer Klete* to be unlocked, and its contents distributed in certain ratio among them. Great was the joy of the village that night. The next morning they presented this paper of happy promise to the *Disponent*. He looked insolently at them—put his hand into his pocket, and pulled out—not the keys of the granary—but another similar piece of paper from the *Hakenrichter*, countermanding the first. The simple men, in the exultation of their hearts, had not remarked that as they came out of one door of the *Hakenrichter's* house, the *Disponent* went in at another, where it cost him but little trouble to persuade that worthy dignitary that he had been, what his vanity most abhorred, and yet invariably incurred, viz., grossly imposed upon.

The village was now in a ferment. The resentment of many was very loud and very safe. Men and women scolded together in a perfect babel of voices, and uttered big threats which were spent in the utterance; but a few there were who said but little, and that little not loud—and these were spirits not to be trifled with.

Mart kept aloof from the whole matter. No one could say that he ever shunned danger or refused help, but he could do nothing here but embroil himself, and his spirit was quenched as he went about his unjust labour with a feeling which was sometimes patience, but oftener desperation.

Meanwhile it had become a matter of difficulty how to maintain even his own reduced household, and ever since Mart's time had been thus taken from him, Anno, originally at Liso's suggestion, had endeavoured to employ her own more profitably.

The good grandmother had to the last spun a finer thread than any other woman in the parish, and, from her, Anno had learnt many a notable little manufacture which finds favour among the higher classes. These she would either commission a neighbour bound for a distant expedition to dispose of for her, or herself, accompanied by a girl from the village, take a day-long walk and sell them at such houses as she could reach.

Mart had known his wife in such safe keeping with his grand-mother, and his thoughts had been so much distracted with other anxieties, that he had relaxed in the vigilance with which he had at first intercepted all attempts on the part of the *Dispo-nent* to approach her. What attempts he had made too — Anno had carefully concealed. She had not told Mart that he had more than once followed her with bad artful words; and that she had always, since that, made a circuit in order to avoid his windows—nor that he had once since the death of Liso, and during the absence of Mart, dared to enter the house, and that she had hidden herself in the empty meal-box till he was gone. Anno was enough of the woman to feel the utmost dread of the villain, and to use every stratagem to avoid him, but too much of the child to take the right means of seeking protection.

The waters had now subsided, and there were those few days of suspense in Nature when the earth, as if just emerged from a chrysalis covering, lies motionless beneath the fresh warmth and light, waiting for strength to expand its wings. Anno had been out the whole day on one of her lace-selling expeditions, and Mart had returned home earlier than usual from the dis-tillery. He found the house at Sellenküll deserted, and expect-ing Anno every instant, who was more than commonly late, he set off walking to meet her.

Anno had gone alone this time without Mart's knowledge, for it was an understood thing that he forbade her ever venturing unaccompanied. But habit had made her bolder. The interval of thaw, when no one can stir, had reduced their meal, and in-creased her stock of lace; and though her usual companion could not go with her, yet she thought the day too fine to be lost. The walk was very far, but quite successful, and she retraced her steps homeward with a light heart. She took the usual *détour* to avoid the *Disponent's* windows; but as she emerged

again on the road between his house and the *Hof,* she observed
that a man's figure was following. She walked quick—the man
gained upon her. Like a frightened hare she ran, and he ran
too. Anno relied upon finding some workmen among the farming buildings that surrounded the great house, but the same
reason that had released Mart earlier had also sent them all home.
Not a soul was there. The buildings stood confusedly together.
She turned a corner, was out of sight of her pursuer for a moment, and dashing through an open doorway into a kind of wood-
house, hid herself among the loose timbers and logs.

She heard the steps pass by—drew herself deeper and deeper
into her place of concealment, and shifted the boards noiselessly
till they covered her more effectually. After some minutes the
footsteps approached again—Anno's heart beat visibly through
her woollen jacket;—they entered the house—searched on all
sides—moved some of the wood till it fell roughly upon her—
had it broken a limb she would not have uttered a sound—and
after keeping her on the stretch of terror for minutes longer
than ever minutes were before, a coarse voice she knew too well
uttered an oath, and the steps left the building. Anno remained
without movement; listening breathless to every sound. There
was perfect silence. Once again she heard the steps—then again
they ceased.

Anno waited and waited there in her constrained position till
an hour seemed to have elapsed. Then cautiously and by de-
grees she crept forward, moved every impediment with as
much fear and precaution as if she had been a culprit escaping
from prison, and at length stood free. With the instinct of self-
defence she took up a log of wood cut ready for firing. With
this in her hand she stealthily emerged—looked to right and to
left, and was just going to plunge into the wide world before
her, when the door of the wood-house, which had laid back apparently against the wall, was flung forward, and the *Disponent*
seized her by the arm.

Anno screamed!—a shrill scream which echoed through the
buildings.

"Yes! you may scream," said Ian insolently; "there is no
one to hear. I have caught you now!" and then changing his
tone,

"So you were stealing the wood—were you? taken in the fact : come you home with me," and he dragged her along. The poor girl screamed, and wept, and struggled, and begged. The *Disponent* only dragged her the faster. All of a sudden, as if an angel from heaven had swept down to her rescue, there came a sound of rushing steps and hard-pent indignant breath, and in a moment Mart's strong fist grasped the *Disponent's* collar.

"Wretch! Villain!" said the young peasant—his lips quivering with fury. "Let go my wife—this moment—let her go."

The *Disponent* turned like a savage; he let go Anno, and at the same time aimed a blow at Mart's face. The young man warded it off.

"She is a thief," said Ian.

"You lie," said Mart, and shook him fiercely.

Then the *Disponent* called her something worse. Mart rolled his eyes wildly around him; snatched the billet of wood which remained unconsciously in Anno's grasp, and still holding his enemy by the collar, poured blow after blow upon his shoulders.

Ian was a great muscular man, and he struggled and fought tremendously; but the pent-up flood had burst—Mart's fury had become frenzy, and his strength was as that of a maniac. He ceased not till it was spent, and then flinging the wretch from him, who staggered upon his feet, he threw the billet after him.

"There! come near my wife again, if you dare."

"Hurrah!" said a voice behind him. "Hurrah! Mart—well done!" and the *Brautwerber* stood a few paces from the scene.

The *Disponent* turned round, gnashed his teeth, and shook his fist. "You shall both smart for this," he said, and hobbled away.

Not a word was spoken as the couple returned to Sellenküll. Mart knew well what he had done, but also knew that had every punishment and torture which the malice of a Russian can devise, been the penalty, he could not and would not have done otherwise. He might rue the deed, but he could never repent it. That evil he most dreaded, and the fear of which had so long disturbed his peace, might come upon him; he was more at peace with himself than he had been for months. Alas! he knew not how soon it would again depart from him!

The next morning he went to work as usual ; and before he returned in the evening, knew that he was sentenced to the utmost penalty which Livonian landholders are permitted to inflict on their peasants—that being the utmost human strength can bear—in other words, to receive forty blows from a club.

The *Brautwerber* was to receive twenty, as a participator in intent, if not in deed—the sentence to be carried into effect three days from this time, in a place most exposed to view in the village.

It is painful now to look into that house at Sellenküll, so long the residence of peace, happiness, and piety. Anno had wept till she was weary. Never before had she known such a weight of woe. Sorrow, dread, and bitter remorse distracted her by turns. She dared not speak to her husband, and when she did lift up her eyes to his face she saw an expression which smote her heart worse than all beside. It was not of unkindness towards herself—that would have been a relief—she would have lowered herself to the dust before him ; but it was a hard, stern, rebellious look, that restrained all anger—suffered no sympathy, and was laying waste all that was good and tender within. His short-lived peace was gone. It supported him in the moment of triumph, but failed before the approach of degradation. Anno watched for a moment to relieve her full heart, and soften his— to ease her heavy weight, by helping to bear his ; but it came not, and she had no strength whilst he had a wrong one. For Mart went on doggedly with his stated employments, as if while he kept up the outer mechanism of his life as usual, no one should dare question what was passing within. Deep commiseration have we with those whose duty is appointed to break the hard heart before they can make way for the comfort they long to give it. Few have the courage or the power—and poor Anno had not.

" Oh ! that Liso had been alive ! she would have known how to reach his heart ; but I, wretched that I am, have brought all this misery upon him, and now cannot help him to bear it." And thus the poor girl lamented, while Mart again went forth silent to his labour.

Meanwhile the ferment in the village had apparently subsided; but we have said there were a few spirits, deep but not loud,

who were not to be trifled with. These had laid a plan, and
now kept it. And early in that same day the *Bauer Klete* was
broken open and forcibly entered

It was empty!

Mart was at his work in the distillery. He had been employed in heating a huge vat sunk into the ground, and rising
about four feet above it, which stood in a kind of open shed, and
was now filling the air with steam. The road from the *Bauer
Klete* led past the distillery. As he replenished the fire, which
was reached from a cavity in the earth on one side, a party of
peasants came up. Their looks and language were those of injured reckless men. They were the same party who had just
broken open the granary. Mart asked them why they were not
at work, for their labour lay in a perfectly opposite direction ;
and they told him in few but meaning words what it was they
had been about. The men were desperate, and they spoke to a
kindred spirit.

At this moment the *Disponent* came up. He looked into the
boiling vat, and down into the fire, and ordered Mart to bring
more wood. The wood lay in another shed about fifty yards off.
Mart obeyed, but lingered, and looked behind. The *Disponent*
was ordering the men off to their work with violent gestures.
Many voices answered ; but one voice, higher than the rest, told
him that he had emptied the granary : and he in return swore at
them, and told them they had stolen the corn themselves. Mart
went on a step, and looked back again. There was a scuffle—
men struggling—the steam obscured the scene for an instant :
then he saw again. The *Disponent* was in the midst of them ;
—he was off his feet,—and oh ! God of Heaven ! they were
forcing him into the boiling vat !

The Tempter whispered at Mart's injured heart, " Let him
die." The heart listened, leapt, and resisted. Swift as a
thought he was in the centre of the struggle. The wretched
man was almost doubled over the edge of the vat ; his hands
clinging to the brazen rim, as if they should sever from his body
sooner than quit hold ; his teeth clenched in the arm of a stout
thickset man, who was putting forth his whole strength, his
head against the *Disponent's* body, to heave him in. It was the
same peasant who had drawn first at the recruiting time. Others

were pushing up his legs ; one was beating the hands, to make them let go ; another was forcing back the head, which still clung by the teeth. In another moment he must have been over. His strength was marvellous, but fruitless ; when the strength of another came to his succour, and Mart's iron grasp was over all. He tore him down to his feet again ; for his onset had been sudden, and the force of ten men, or rather of a righteous cause, was in him. "Maddis!—brethren!—would ye be murderers? Let the villain live! The devil will have his own soon enough." The men relinquished their hold. The *Disponent* stood in their midst with bleeding face and hands, and torn clothes : then they opened a way for him, and with jeers and hootings drove him from the shed. He turned a look of diabolical intent—clenched his bloody fist at them—mounted his horse with difficulty—beat the animal about the head, till it broke into a furious gallop, and went off in the direction of the *Hakenrichter*.

Mart now left the shed till the men had dispersed. He was too proud and too generous to speak to one of them of what had happened. He would have been ashamed to have received a word of praise, or to have heard a word of contrition, for he knew how hard and desperate his own heart had been.

His thoughts were bewildered ; the dreadful struggle that had just passed before him—the violent passions he had witnessed and felt, suspended for a while the sense of what had been and what was to come. But as these gradually subsided, the punishment that awaited him seemed for the first time to fall on his spirit with its whole fearful reality. Till now he had had something within him stronger even than the dread of degradation—the pride of a rebellious heart : now that had given way, and Mart's punishment was to take place on the morrow!

He stood on the same spot where the battle for life and death had just been fought ; and he knew how great was his misery, for he could have welcomed the death the other had escaped ; nay, he felt for a moment as if he could have sought it.

We have no right to search further into the feelings of the much-tried man. There are secret passions in each nature hidden even to our own knowledge, till some circumstance out of the course of that nature calls them forth, either to be crushed in their birth or to live to our destruction. The common foes and the common trials of this life are the only fair tests by which a good man should be judged, and not a monstrous conjuration of adversity, long the terror of his imagination, and now suddenly realized to his senses, like this which hung over poor Mart. It was a moral phantom before which the ordinary strength and courage of a man may quail, without any reproach to his manliness or to his religious principles.

Meanwhile the change seemed to affect body as well as mind. The strong hands trembled ; the muscular limbs refused to put forth their power. It was well the *Disponent* did not return as usual, for Mart could not work. He wore out the day as he had never worn out one before, not even with the terrors of the recruitage before him, and set off for home earlier than usual.

Mart and the *Brautwerber* had not met since their respective sentences had reached them. At first he had purposely kept aloof. Now he felt as if he would gladly have looked him in the face—or seen him, himself unseen—though to exchange a word on the subject nearest each heart he felt would be beyond his power, and, upon any other, a kind of mockery. While he mused thus he saw the two well-known figures approaching— the stooping father and the puny child. Mart stood irresolute what to do, but Juhann decided the matter ; as he drew near he crossed to the other side of the road, averting his face. Mart saw that he avoided him. He stood looking after his poor friend with a bleeding heart. The figure had something so joyless and hopeless in it ; yet he walked quickly, almost wildly so, till the little feet ran unequally at his side.

That evening the husband and wife mingled their sorrow. Mart's heart had thrown off all disguise and restraint. He permitted sympathy ; he asked advice ; he begged forgiveness ; he showed despair. Anno had never seen him thus utterly prostrate in spirit before, and it seemed to advance her years in thought and courage. He told her, for his heart could keep nothing on it, of the dreadful scene of the morning ; how nearly murder had been committed amongst them, and of the temptation he had felt to permit it. And Anno listened with kindling eyes.

"Oh, Mart ! surely he must let you off now. You saved his life !"

Mart shook his head.

"Is he a man like other men, Anno? No; he is a *Disponent*: neither mercy nor gratitude was ever known to him. No, no—those poor fellows will suffer next. Oh, God! what shall we all do." Then changing his tone with a bitterness quite foreign to his nature: "I see how it will all be, Anno; to-morrow ——;" and he shut his eyes as if to exclude the picture. "Next week we turn out of our house, and next autumn I shall be taken for a recruit: that will be the end of us:" and he walked up and down in a state of mind sad and fearful to witness.

That night Anno was kept awake with many thoughts. Mart had not slept since his sentence had reached him. She heard his deep sighs and restless movements during the first watches of the night; then he fell into a deep slumber: but his little wife never closed her eyes.

H

CHAPTER XI.

MART slept sound and late, and the sun was far higher in the heavens than usual when he arose. It was not a distillery day: that was why Anno had not waked him; but he knew what day it was, and the mind resumed its weight instantly, and felt it the heavier for the short respite it had enjoyed. Anno was not in the house; she was doubtless without, for the door stood wide open, and let in a gleam of sunshine. Then Mart heard a step. He turned to look for her, but a smaller shadow darkened the threshold, and Juhann's little boy entered. Mart looked at the child with surprise.

" Where 's your father?"

" Gone back again," said the little meek voice.

" But what are you come for, little Juhann?"

" Father told me to come. He brought me, but not all the way; I walked alone from the bridge:" and the little fellow said this with great satisfaction.

Mart did not know what to make of all this. He called Anno, but no answer came. He looked round the house— 'twas evident she had left it.

He then questioned the child again, but little pale Juhann never wavered from his tale—his father had brought him part of the way, and gone home again. He had bid him come on straight to Mart's house, and tell him he had sent him. The child carried a little dirty bundle. Mart looked into it: it contained a few squalid articles of Livonian childhood's attire. Mart's mind misgave him with an undefined fear. He stood undecided for an instant; then he took out bread and milk, and gave it to the child; told him not to leave the house; gave him in charge to Karria Pois, who perfectly understood the commission and laid down at the open door; and then set off quickly for the *Brautwerber's* dwelling.   Anno's absence puzzled him, but he did not think of that now.

It was a most exquisite morning, combining the freshness of dawn with the brightness of noonday; and both acting upon the hidden treasures of the earth with the resistless force and wondrous speed of a northern spring.   All vegetable life was obeying the call.   The grass leapt up at once from its brown bed into soft straight spikes hardly steady on their feet.   The tender swollen buds of the shrubs and deciduous trees threw open leaf after leaf, crowding one before the other, till the innermost saw the light; and the coarse rinds and tough barks of the hardier fir and pine tribes began to move with an inner life, and broke out into joyous stirring sounds, as if thankful to emancipate what they had so long and tightly covered.

It was fortunate our poor Mart was not given to moralizing, or the joyousness of all around might have sharpened the despondency within.   Still he felt something of this, though indistinctly, as his eyes saw the fresh verdure and his nostrils breathed the balmy air, and his heart carried a heavy load!   A vague sense of foreboding urged him on, and he quickened his steps till he came within sight of Juhann's house.   It lay in full sunshine; all still and peaceful around it.   Mart stood on the threshold and looked in at the first chamber.   No one was there.   He called: no one answered.   He went through into the inner room, and more than his worst fears were at once realized— Juhann's body hung lifeless behind the door!

The body was warm as in life, though perfectly dead.   Mart girded up his feelings with a strong will; took it down; laid it on the wretched bed, and covered up the face he shuddered to look on.   Then he cast himself on his knees beside it, and first came groans of anguish, and then bitter tears, as the young man poured forth his oppressed and afflicted soul in fervent prayer to his Maker.   The tyranny he had struggled under had now borne its worst fruit.   The oppressor had now doubly sinned—in himself and in his victim.   For who could arraign that mute helpless clay for the act that had made it so!   Mart knew that the soul of his poor friend was guiltless of its own enfranchisement. He knew that the guardian spirit must have deserted its sacred temple, ere the pious patient sufferer would have lifted a hand

H 2

to demolish it.   But he! he had murmured against the will of
the Most High with a clear reason and a sound understanding;
and as the recollection of his own proud and rebellious spirit rose
up before him, he felt that his crime was far the heavier of the
two.   It was true he was called upon to bear what he had most
dreaded to encounter, and most prayed to be spared; but was
there not One who had given His cheek to the scorners, and His
shoulders to the smiters!   In His strength would he take up his
cross and follow Him: and though his spirit might recoil, it
should no longer rebel.

Long did the young man remain prostrate before the remains
of the friend he had loved so well; then he arose with a broken
and a contrite heart, and gazed mournfully upon them.   The body
lay there so weary and worn out, as if life had been one perpetual task, and death its first moment of ease.   To all the springs
of joy and hope it had died years before, and the mortal machine
had pressed heavy on the spirit without them.   Those limbs had
never been eased of their toil by one elastic bound of the mind;
and what human limbs will not give way, thus left to labour
alone!

Poor Juhann!   Mart's surmises were his just due.   The re-
currence of the same sentence that had first broken his spirit had
now finally overturned it.   His reason, which the long settled
melancholy of years had been insensibly undermining, had begun
to waver on her seat from the moment he had received the tidings of his punishment: and as the time for its accomplishment
drew nigh, had finally left him a prey to the wild suggestions of
a disordered mind.   Yet it is a sweet though sad lesson in the
sorrowful page of human infirmity, to know that in all the per-
versions and distortions of the poor mental machine, thus left to
its own misrule, the love for his child kept true to its place.   He
had deliberately brought the child to his friend's house; he had
consciously left it there with the conviction that that friend would
redeem his trust; and then, having thus taken precautions which
acted doubly for his intended purpose, he had hastened home with
the self-gratulating cunning of a maniac, and committed the deed.

Peace be to his spirit!   Mart felt that it was an invisible
witness, as he took the sinewless and now fast chilling hand in
his, and vowed a solemn vow that henceforth the child should be

dear to his heart as his own, and precious in his eyes as the last
bequest of a loved and murdered friend. Then he turned to
leave the house of death and seek the little orphan.

But first he must give tidings of the event in the village, and
send a messenger to inform the pastor. As he closed the door of
the house a fellow-peasant met him, and hastily inquired where
was the *Disponent*, for that the pastor wanted him. He was
not in the field, nor at the *Hof*, nor in his own house, and
nobody had seen him : Mart had not seen him either ; but he
thought in his heart that he would be found at the *Hakenrichter's*, giving deposition of the yesterday's occurrence, if he
had not given it before ; and if not there, he knew too well
that by a certain hour that afternoon he would be sure to
make his appearance. But he said nothing ; and hearing the
pastor was in the village, he gave the man the sorrowful tidings
to convey to him, and turned his own face homeward. Anno's
and little Juhann's eyes were all that should meet his till the fatal
hour arrived. When he reached Sellenküll, the child sat upon
the threshold, and Karria Pois by it wagging his great tail ; but
Anno was still absent.

We must now follow her in the mingled affairs of this day.
Anno had risen early that morning, bent on executing plans
which the silent hours of the night had ripened in her mind. She
had immediately seen to what advantage Mart's noble conduct of
the previous day could be turned in his favour, if made known in
the right quarter. Her plan was therefore simply this ; to go to
the pastor, inform him of the whole affair from beginning to end,
and either beg him to accompany her to the *Hakenrichter*, or
leave him to undertake the cause alone, as he might think best.
Hakenrichter or not *Hakenrichter*—Russian or not Russian—she
felt assured he must have a heart of some kind ; only *Disponents*
had none. As for this latter, the reflection of the night had con-
vinced her that Mart was right in expecting nothing from his
gratitude : nay, like a true woman, when once she admits conviction at all, she went further still, and doubted whether Ian would
not even forego his second vengeance for a few hours, so as the
more securely to satisfy the first. Then the men themselves, as
long as he aid not speak, would be too much interested in concealing their frightful attempt to mention how it had been pre-

vented.   In short, there was no one who could stir in the matter
but herself, and no time to lose, for four o'clock was the dreaded
hour.   She had deliberated much whether she should ask Mart's
leave to consult the pastor—she had asked it when the sentence
first came, and had been sternly denied—she dared not ask
again now, lest she should meet with the same answer; at the
same time he had not bound her to secrecy, therefore she was
free : still it was a bold act to do, and sometimes she walked
quicker, sometimes slower, as doubts came and went in her mind.
Then she thought the pastor would advise for the best.   If he
approved, no one could do otherwise, and she walked steadily on.

She passed the great mansion and through the farming buildings with a heavy heart, and took the usual round to avoid the
Disponent's windows ; but she saw from a distance that his horse,
saddled and bridled, was feeding down by the stream, and fearing he would soon be coming out, she hastened her steps.   It was
a long nine wersts' walk to the *Pastorat*, and Anno was thankful
when she saw the church tower.   Nevertheless she felt a little
flurried with what was before her when she reached the back door
of the humble wooden building and inquired for the "*Pastor
Erra.*"   But she felt indescribably worse on receiving for answer
that the pastor had just driven away on one of his parish rounds,
and would not be home till late in the afternoon.   Anno's heart
sunk within her ; the stay and comfort of her whole purpose was
gone ; she felt worse than forsaken ; she felt, at first, as if she
was guilty.   The colour mounted crimson under her cap, and
she sat down on a bench, hardly knowing what to think, far less
what to do.

But Anno was not required to think.   Such plans, once set
agoing in the mind, have a life and action of their own.   An
unlooked for interruption like this may shake and unsettle them
for a while ; but if we only wait patiently, they adapt themselves
into fresh forms, seemingly without any agency of ours.

Anno had not sat there many minutes before she found what
she had to do.   The pastor's absence had not altered one argument for her mission ; it had only taken away all that had made
it easy to herself.   It was too late to have her husband's leave or
advice now, and she had rather never see him again than go
back and confess that her heart had failed her in the task, merely

because she found it more difficult than she had expected. At first the thought crossed her that she would follow the pastor to the village; but there she would meet people, or even Mart might see her, or she might miss the pastor after all, and lose precious time. No; it was plain she must go on to the *Haken-richter's* alone. Anno had never heard either of Elizabeth of Siberia or of Jeannie Deans; but something of the spirit of both was in her, as she rose from her seat with a further walk of seven wersts before her, and the dreadful *Hakenrichter* at the end of it.

In truth Anno's mission was now by no means an easy one; for to all appearance the chief argument for saving Mart from punishment could not be fully brought forward without putting others in jeopardy of the same; but this she was resolved nothing should induce her to do. Come what might, the names of the men who had made the attempt on the *Disponent* should not pass her lips; otherwise she made no plan of what she was to say, and thought with dismay of the pastor's superior eloquence. But she was resolved not to care for any bullyings or cross-questionings that might await her, for she felt nothing could confuse her in her story—she had only the truth to tell—though she might not tell the whole of it. Not but she was assailed by fits of terror regarding her probable reception by the *Hakenrichter*, and also possible encounter with the *Disponent* either there or on the road, but the one great anxiety for Mart soon bore all lesser ones down; she looked up to the sun, saw it high in the heavens, and rested not till the great house was before her.

Here she was confronted with the awful object of her journey sooner than she had expected; for the *Hakenrichter* himself was walking up the road accompanied by a young man Anno had never seen before. They would have taken no notice of her " *terra ommegast,*" or good morning, but she stopped straight before them, made that supplicatory action with her hands which we have mentioned before, and stood still.

" What do you want, woman?" said the *Hakenrichter* with his terrific voice : " get you gone—what do you want?"

Anno meekly answered that she wanted to speak with the *Hakenrichter Erra.*

" Nonsense, you don't want ; I'm busy, can't you see ? Come another time."   And then he turned to the stranger, and with a most urbane voice began to explain that the office of *Hakenrichter* was one of incessant toil and trouble, and that no one in the province performed it so punctiliously as himself.

" But can't you speak to this poor girl ?" said the young man, who had remarked Anno's anxious and wistful expression, and was looking with interest at her pretty face and person.

" Oh ! 'tis all nonsense ; only some got-up tale : one must not encourage these *canaille*.   Where do you come from, woman ?"

Anno gave the name of the estate, and the *Hakenrichter* burst out laughing, and said in German, " From Essmegghi !—one of your own sheep, *Herr Baron* ! You'll have enough of it soon. Well ! well ! go in and wait."

Anno went in and sat silent in the *Volkstube*.   In about half an hour she was summoned into an inner room.   Her heart did beat terribly, for now the time was come, and all depended on her.   The *Hakenrichter* was seated on a divan smoking a cigar ; the stranger was standing by the window.   The sight of him was an encouragement to her ; for women, children, and the unfortunate—and Anno was all three—have an instinct for knowing their friends.

The *Hakenrichter* looked up, saw that it was a very pretty young girl standing before him, and addressed her in tones very different to those he had at first adopted, but which Anno liked still less.   But he wished to appear both humane and witty in the eyes of his companion, and was under the impression that an insolent familiarity exactly combined the two.

" Well, my pretty maid ! what are you come for ? Do you want me to get you a husband ?"

" I am married," said Anno quietly, pointing to the matron's cap on her head, as if that was all-sufficient proof.

" Oh ! you are married ! are you ?   That 's stupid of you ; husbands are troublesome things for such pretty girls as you. Here—let me hear all about it—come closer."

But Anno neither answered a word nor stirred an inch.   The *Hakenrichter* went on in the same strain, and she turned a distressed and a modest look to the young man at the window.   He had listened to the whole, and now came forward with a gesture of impatience.

"Let the poor woman speak, *Herr Hakenrichter;* I should like to hear what she has to say. What did you come for, my good girl?" he said encouragingly.

"I came to speak about my husband," said Anno.

"And who is your husband?"

"He is a three-day peasant on the Essmegghi *mois.*"

"What's his name?" said the *Hakenrichter* in a voice of authority, as if he thought it time for him to interfere.

"Mart Addafer," said Anno.

"Mart Addafer!" said the *Hakenrichter.* "Mart Addafer! Why, isn't that the fellow who beat the *Disponent!* Isn't that the man who's to be flogged for it to-day?" A deep painful flush overspread Anno's face and throat.

"He's a lazy insolent dog," said the *Hakenrichter* to his companion. "He beat the *Disponent* because he caught him stealing wood. He's the worst peasant on the whole estate."

"Oh, no! no!" said Anno vehemently, "that's not true; not one word. My husband never stole wood—he is not lazy. Oh! let me speak—pray let me speak;" and she clasped her hands and came forward with passionate entreaty. And she did speak. Words poured out, quick and eager, the abundance of a woman's heart. She told them that the *Disponent* was her husband's enemy, and that he had sought every opportunity to injure him. She related how he had defrauded him of his gains, and taxed him with unjust work, and exposed him to the risk of the recruitage, and summoned him to leave his house : and how the whole parish had suffered ; and how the *Disponent* had prevented the *Bauer Klete* from being thrown open—and no wonder ; and then she found she was getting on to dangerous ground, and she suddenly stopped.

"But what has made the *Disponent* so particularly your husband's enemy?" said the stranger. It would have been more logical, certainly, if Anno had begun with this part of the story ; though the absence of plan vouched the more for its truth with any who could understand what truth was. But she wanted the help of a question, as all untaught speakers do.

And now, with a change of manner and with a downcast eye,

as if the eagerness to speak had given way to a consciousness of what she was saying, she related the rather extraordinary mistake on her part, which had given rise to Ian's ill will—though why he kept it up so virulently she could not tell—for Mart never injured or provoked him; but still she knew this was the reason why he was so hard upon them, and so did Mart; and she told them how he would not allow her to work at the *Disponent's* house, but had paid a woman for her, and how he had laboured to maintain his own household and help his neighbours during this severe winter; and how there was nobody to be compared to Mart, for that he was always industrious and always kind, and but for him many more would have been starved to death; and she was going off eloquently in this direction, when another question brought her up, and again the eyes were cast down, and she owned that the *Disponent* had never ceased to persecute her, and had said many wrong things to her—more than Mart knew; and how he had once come into her house, and how she always took a round to avoid his windows; and finally she described the scene in the wood-house, and how the *Disponent* was dragging her away to his house, when Mart heard her scream, and came up.

"And what did your husband do?" said the young man, who had never taken his eyes off her.

"Mart beat him," said Anno with a little hesitation.

"But," she added eagerly, "Mart never stole any wood. He only took the piece that was in my hand, and that," said the poor girl, "he threw after him."

There was a short pause, and Anno stood, with quick breath and eye, looking from one to the other; a burning crimson spot fastened high upon each cheek. "What a villain that man is!" said the stranger. "Thank God I am back!"

The *Hakenrichter* burst into a loud laugh. "You don't believe all this story, do you, *Herr Baron?* They'll impose on you easy enough."

The Baron turned quick to Anno, and said sharply, "Woman! is all this true that you have been telling us? Is it all true?"

"True?" said Anno solemnly; "true?—yes. Lies could not have given me strength to come here." And again there was a pause.

" And what do you want the *Hakenrichter* to do for you ?"

Anno clasped her hands. She had given her story eloquently, but the end and object of it all still remained behind ; and now she saw but little encouragement on that hard ugly face.

" Oh ! the *Erra* knows what I want. The *Erra* can send me home a happy woman. My husband is not guilty—he is not a bad man. He is the best man in the parish, if I dared to tell you all. Oh ! *Erra !* you have heard my words—you would not punish an innocent man ! It will ruin him for life. He 'll never look up again after it, and it will break my heart !" And tears for the first time began to trickle down her cheeks.

The Baron rose up with an angry and disturbed gesture.

" Pooh, nonsense !" said the *Hakenrichter*, puffing his cigar ; "none of this—not so easy to break your hearts. How do I know this is true ?"

" Oh ! it is true, all true," said Anno passionately ; "and more, if I dared to speak."

" You must let the poor man off," said the baron imperatively.

" But it can't be done," said the *Hakenrichter*, fast rising into a passion. The sentence is written down ; it has passed through the *Gouvernement's Regierung* already. You know nothing about *Hakenrichter's* business."

" But I know truth from falsehood," said the young man, kindling too. " And you don't pretend the laws here punish a man, whether he is guilty or no, merely because his sentence is written down."

" 'T is a parcel of nonsense," said the *Hakenrichter ;* "I can't be humbugged by a fool of a girl. What business had a fellow like her husband to beat a *Disponent ?* He deserves a flogging for it. What 's a beating to him ? They don't feel it. I dare say he has had plenty before now."

" Never ! never !" cried Anno, interrupting the stranger, who, boiling with indignation, was about to speak. " Oh ! *Erra, Erra*, I have more to say. I 'll tell you all. *Erra*, the *Disponent* is a wicked man—a very wicked man. He ought to be begging here himself for my husband's pardon, instead of leaving me to do it. He ought, indeed ; for Mart saved his life only yesterday. He saved him only yesterday, when the men would have thrown him into the boiling vat. He alone saved him."

"What men?" said the *Hakenrichter*, his eyes gleaming.

"Oh! *Erra;* the *Bauer Klete* was empty—quite empty, and they were starving men, and their children are dying. And he angered them when they could bear no more; and it was in the distillery!"

"What! they tried to throw him into the boiling vat?" said the stranger with horror.

"Oh! they knew not what they did. But Mart saved him— he alone; though God knows Ian has injured him more than he has done any other, much more, and is now letting him be beaten unjustly." And she covered her face with her hands and sobbed piteously.

"How dreadful this is! What a disgraceful, infamous state of things!" said the stranger. "But it is my fault."

And then he drew from Anno, as soon as she had recovered herself, a more coherent account of the matter; learnt how the resources of the *Bauer Klete* had been denied to them during the whole of that dreadful winter; and again, when their need was past bearing: how some of the peasants—but her Mart was not of the number—had broken it open in their desperation—had found it robbed of its contents, and knew who alone could have done it.

"But are you sure," said the young man, trying to be very cautious, "that the peasants had not really robbed it themselves? —perhaps at some earlier period in the winter, when they were hard pressed," he added, as if to induce her to confess. But Anno answered, that it was easy for those to think so who had not seen the misery of those who were alive, nor felt the light coffins of those who were gone. The young man shuddered. If they had stolen the corn, what had they done with it? No—the *Disponent* always kept the key, and it was plain enough now, why he was so unwilling to have it put into the door. This was only one of his many acts of dishonesty. When their own *Erra* came home, he would find plenty.

Anno was too much pre-occupied to observe the odd expression that came over her hearer's face, who now went on to question her, and heard how the *Disponent* had come across them when their passions were thus excited, and threatened and abused them for the very thing he had done himself, as he had often done before, she said, with impunity, and might have done now, if the boiling vat had not been just at hand.

"And who were the men?" said the *Hakenrichter*; "tell me their names."

Anno answered nothing.

"What are their names?" he repeated.

Anno shook her head.

He did not urge her further, though, whether withheld by some better feelings latent in his breast, or by his companion's rising indignation, or by the recollection that he should hear it all in due time from the *Disponent*, we must leave——

"What signify their names," said the stranger hastily; "I only wonder they did not murder him outright," he added in German. And then he went on speaking emphatically in that language.

By this time the reader has perceived that the young man was the proprietor of Essmegghi, and, therefore, entitled to urge his request for the immediate remission of Mart's punishment. The peasants were his dependants; the *Disponent* his servant. He had returned suddenly, and gone to the nearest proprietor's abode, as is the custom in this country of widely scattered population.

The *Hakenrichter* now took a slip of paper, wrote upon it, read it, sanded it, shook it, and finally handed it to Anno.

"Here, woman! Give this to the *Disponent* from me, and tell your husband he may stop at home this afternoon."

Anno glanced at the paper, which was Greek to her, and looked from the *Hakenrichter* to the baron with a look of breathless inquiry.

"'T is your husband's pardon," said the *Hakenrichter*; "tell him that if"— he was going to add some *Hakenrichter*-kind of advice for his future better conduct, when his hands were seized and kissed one after the other, and his sleeve was kissed, and the tail of his coat was kissed: and then Anno flew and performed the same operation upon the stranger; said that Jummal would bless them, and that she should love them, and then stood holding the paper with such a grateful glistening face as none could possibly preach to. But still she stood.

"You want something more," said the young man. "Come —what is it?"

Yes. Anno did want something more, and could not be happy without it. She had not forgotten the poor *Brautwerber*, though she had been tactician enough not to bring his cause forward before. But now she told them simply and artlessly how little the unoffending man had done to deserve such punishment, and that her husband would not be happy, though he was let off himself.

"And what is his punishment down for—for stealing wood too?" said the Baron. "You must reverse this as well, *Herr Hakenrichter*, for all the *Gouvernement's Regierung*, may say." That gentleman replied nothing, but began writing again; and Anno saw that all was right.

Then the Baron came up to her with a kind voice and face, and told her that he was glad to have such a good couple on his estate, for that he was their own *Erra*, and was come to live among them, and would take care of her and her husband, and not let them be removed from their house. And Anno did not know what to do for joy; she exhausted all her forms of national acknowledgment, and still had her heart as full as ever, and said that Mart would thank him, and Mart would serve him. And then the baron praised what she had done, and called her a faithful little wife, and she put down her head, and was her own bashful Livonian self again.

"Here's the other paper," said the Baron. I don't think you'll lose them, will you?"

" *Ei, ei* "—No, no, said Anno, blushing.

" Nor lose any time on the road. But it is a long way; you'll be tired."

Mitte nilt"—not now, said Anno, smiling and blushing; and she left the room.

Who does not know the happiness of retracing with a light and a hopeful heart the same path over which you have recently carried it heavy and anxious? The sense of release from pain added to that of the presence of joy. Anno looked at every roadside object with a sort of special exultation. They had seen her pass sorrowing, now they saw her return rejoicing, and she felt grateful to each one in turn, for they seemed to remind her of past sufferings only the more to enhance the fullness of present bliss ! She did not know she was tired though her feet began

involuntarily to slacken, or if she did, there was a fresh sense of
pleasure in feeling that it was only the body that was weary.
Not a care nor an anxiety to give a false strength, while that of
the physical frame was being exhausted, and to withdraw all
support when that was gone.

Anno saw by the sun that it was about the second hour past
noon. She was now on her own ground again, and fast approaching the *Disponent's* house. She debated within herself
whether she should at once take the precious paper to him ; but
the dread of meeting him, however his powers of injury might
be curtailed, as well as the secret wish to show the paper herself
first to Mart, made her resolve in the negative. There would be
time enough for Mart to deliver it himself, and Anno wished for
no more independent doings. As she drew near the house
her resolution was confirmed ; for two or three peasants stood at
the door, and she saw there was a bustle, as of many people
within.

This part of her road behind her, her whole heart expanded
with the excess of happiness she was bringing. It was not only
release from present disgrace, it was assurance of future protection, security to continue in their home, freedom from recruitage—a boundless vista !—and as she crossed her own threshold, so
much emotion and fatigue had nearly deprived her of utterance.

Mart was sitting within ; the child upon his knee ; himself
looking almost as broken-spirited as the father it had just lost,
yet with a placid expression which showed that his manly heart
had found comfort and strength even with the dreaded trial full
in view. Anno's hasty entrance and flurried look made him
start up with anxiety.

" Anno ! what is it ? Where have you been ?" Anno could
not speak a word. Love and joy, and bashful pride, and excessive weariness of body, all overpowered her at once, and the
little woman fell all strengthless before him, and was soon seated
where little Juhann had just been, her head on his shoulder,
telling in broken accents all she had ventured and all she had
obtained.

" Mart ! do you forgive me ?"

" My Anno—my Anno !" And husband and wife said but
few words, but exchanged feelings many a higher born couple

might have envied.   " And Juhann too, poor fellow ! I did not forget him," said Anno, all smiles.

Mart's face fell.

" You need not look so distressed, Mart.   See here, I have his pardon too !" and she held up the second paper.

" Anno ! he needs another pardon now," said Mart solemnly. " Man can no longer hurt nor help him."   And he told the sad tale.

Then Anno felt that unalloyed joy was not to be our portion here below ; and thoughts visited her young mind which had never found entrance there before.   All the selfishness of her happiness had passed away.

She now took the child tenderly, and sat without the door resting herself, while Mart went off to show the token of that release she had purchased for him.

CHAPTER XII.

MEANWHILE we must tell how it went with the good pastor this day, for he too had taken an unlooked-for share in its events. We have said that the consciences of the poor degraded Livonian peasantry are sensitive and tender. They may be as liable to crime as any other set of the human race, but they can less bear its burthen on their hearts. During the course of that morning the pastor received a full confession of the attempt upon the *Disponent's* life from two of the men principally concerned in it. And this without any ulterior hope or object; for they knew how little their poor pastor could help them, and knew not that other help was nigh.

The pastor was inexpressibly shocked; he gave solemn and befitting admonition, but the bruised reed he could not break, and his whole spirit rose up against the tyranny which could thus have incited his pious and long-suffering people to take vengeance from Him to whom it belongs. He felt that further aggravation must be prevented, or that he could not answer for the consequences, nor scarce find it in his heart to blame them; and he sought the *Disponent* strong in the terrors of earthly and spiritual judgments. As we have seen, he did not succeed in finding him, though search was made in various directions of the estate. Then came the intelligence of poor Juhann's fate. The pastor visited the body, and set off immediately for the *Haken-richter's*, where he arrived shortly after Anno had left.

Here the unexpected meeting with the young baron, whom he had known in earlier years, gave immediate pledge for the fulfilment of his object; nevertheless the old man did not relinquish the least part of the duty he had undertaken. He re-

I

capitulated all that Anno had related, and told them that though
the shedding of blood had been mercifully prevented in this
instance, yet that one life had already been sacrificed to the
tyranny that had been permitted, and one soul was already gone
to plead against it at the bar of Heaven.   He then solemnly
arraigned the *Hakenrichter* for all the oppression that had been
practised beneath the shelter of his authority ; reminded him
that he sat in the seat of judgment to show mercy and execute
righteousness, and charged him as a minister of God with having
abused his power to strengthen the bands of wickedness and en-
large the sorrows of adversity.

The *Hakenrichter* was a coward : he quailed beneath the re-
bukes of the humble apostolic man he had affected to despise,
and was at once ready to desert and to punish the wretch his
authority had encouraged.   All idea of earthly retribution, however, was far from the pastor's thoughts, even had it lain within
the compass of the law.   His only aim was to protect his people
from further oppression, by depriving the chief instrument of it
of further power.

It now cost him but little trouble to induce the young baron
to accompany him, and take up his abode at the *Pastorat,* when
he would be close to his own property, and able at once to commence that active personal superintendence which could best
repair the past.   They therefore left the *Hakenrichter* alone with
his shame, if that sense of detection can be so called which such
a mind as his is alone capable of feeling.   As for real shame, it
was only in the breast of the young proprietor that it was to be
found.   He had been carefully and religiously educated in
another and a more favoured land ; and the misery and oppression
which this first day of his return had thus opened upon him,
came sharpened to his heart with self-reproach for the absence
that had thus encouraged it.   As they drove along, he related to
the pastor Anno's visit of the morning, and the interest with
which her tale and manner had inspired him.   The pastor confirmed the report of Mart with affectionate enthusiasm ; but he
knew not till now of the danger in which he had stood ; and even
his charitable nature felt impatient for the moment that should
confront the dishonest steward with his offended master.

They drove therefore at once to the *Disponent's* house.   As

they drew near, many peasants were standing at the door; and
one instantly came forward to meet them.

" What a fine young fellow," exclaimed the baron.

" The very man we were speaking of," answered the pastor.
" Did you ever see a better physiognomy? "

" Well, Mart! is the villain found?"

Mart helped the old man out of his vehicle with a serious face
and manner—then drew him aside, and spoke for a few minutes.
The pastor lifted up his hands in horror and surprise—hastened
into the house, and stood by the bedside of a mangled and a dying
man.

This eventful day had yet brought forth another and more
awful tragedy. While the purposes of man were pursuing the
instrument of so much evil, those of the Most High had over-
taken him. The reader will remember that from the moment
the *Disponent* left the distillery he has nowhere appeared upon
the scene. He left it with feelings of rage and vengeance in his
heart, and these he wantonly poured out upon the animal that
bore him away. The poor horse was like the injured men he
had just quitted—it could bear much, but not beyond a certain
mark. His master continued to beat it cruelly as it carried him
swifter and swifter along, till, in a lonely part, the galled animal
lost patience—plunged, reared, and threw him with violence
from its back. The wretched man fell on his face with tremendous force : a sharp short stake, sticking out of the ground,
entered the eyeball and impaled him there; and his right arm
was broken by the fall. For a time he lay insensible; and,
being concealed among low bushes, was not discovered by the
few who passed that way. Towards night, however, sensibility
returned; and he lay in such agonies as even his most persecuted
victims, hungry and spiritless as they were on their wretched
beds, would have pitied. The horse found its way back to the
house during the night, as Anno had seen ; but as for its brutal
master, in spite of the search made for him, it was not till several
hours later that his groans attracted the attention of a passing
peasant. He summoned others ; and they had just carried him
to his home when Anno passed it on her return. We forbear to
lift the curtain from the last hours of such an offender. He lingered for two days in unspeakable agonies, and died in them;

and the next Sunday saw both him and poor Juhann laid in the ground.

The events of this day produced a great sensation in the parish, and brought forth many traits of character among the want-stricken and degraded peasantry which it was grateful to observe. They saw the finger of God in the *Disponent's* awful end, and looked on with reverence and fear. While he lay on his bed of suffering, there were many who returned him good for evil, by such little services as were in their power ; and when he was gone to his last account, there was no one who triumphed.

Not that it was the immediate relief to their sufferings and the assurance of future care and protection, in the presence of their young master, which tempered their bitterness; on the contrary, his benefits were received with little cordiality, and his presence viewed with indifference. Meanwhile he did all that proprietor could do to repair the past, and that immediately. Food was plentifully distributed ; seed-corn given for immediate tillage ; ground restored that had been alienated ; inquiry instituted ; complaints listened to, and compensation made. But it required both the wisdom of age and the ardour of youth for the young man not to flag and draw back before the prospect which opened itself to him. On the one hand, a set of worn-down impoverished peasants, without any interest or trust in him ; on the other, such plausible or vexatious laws, screening the wicked and entangling the good, as took from him all trust in himself. The baron was by birth and family a native of this country, but he had been, as we have said, brought up far from Russian influence ; and the mystery of her iniquity broke upon him, as it must do upon every foreigner, only in his case more suddenly.

" This poor country seems to lie under a curse," said the Baron, as he and the pastor paced up and down the little *Pastorat* garden.

" Too true," said the old man sorrowfully ; " but it is a curse she has brought upon herself."

" It seems," continued the young man, " as if honesty and singleness of purpose could not live in it; wherever I turn, I find only lying, cheating, and oppression, and these always successful—till my courage fails me."

" It must not," said the pastor. " It is precisely such men as you who should live here, and spread order and confidence around you. Your peasants show you no trust or cordiality. No wonder!—a proprietor is with them only another name for an oppressor. They are stupid enough, poor things! but they would be stupider still if they were to trust you all at once," said the old man, with a dry laugh. " But live among them—cultivate them—show them that you have pleasure in their well-doing, and interest in their trials, and they 'll reward you. They are my only reward, that 's all I know," he added mournfully.

Then continuing : " There 's more to be done with these people than with the real Russians ; and yet I like those fellows too : but these are a more moral and religious people. It is higher classes only, both in these provinces and in Russia, who bring all the sin and misery upon the country."

" But the higher classes of these Provinces are Germans," said the Baron : " I knew what Russia was ; but here, I own, I expected a very different state of affairs." ′

" Ah! that 's the thing. It is true they have German titles and German tongues, but too many are only a bad mixture. They are Germans without Christianity, and Russians without superstition. They have got infidelity from the one country, and barbarity from the other ; and are doubly unfit to rule this people. For my poor peasants are equally removed from either ; a religious people may be poor and silly, but they can't be barbarous. I look forward sometimes with dread to the end of these things," said the old man with a sigh ; " with a ruler too at the head of this monstrous empire who ——. But don't let us talk of these matters : enough for the day is the evil therefore. Only do you not forsake us, *Herr Baron*. There are some few good and humane nobles in the land ; and you and such have much in your own hands, as you will find when you enter more into the affairs of our little province. Meanwhile let us think of the affairs of our little Essmeggi, for you have plenty to do there. You want another man to supply that wretched *Disponent's* place. There 's one I have to recommend, whom I know we shall think alike about."

" I was going to mention the same," said the Baron ; and they continued their walk.

The next day Mart was summoned to the *Pastorat.* When he
returned, his looks and manner bore witness that his errand had
been one of the most agreeable kind ; but his tongue told nothing.   Anno, however, could refrain hers, albeit as curious as
most other women—or men ; but the concealment, whatever it
might be in import, was evidently of a happy nature, and this
she knew would do Mart no harm to keep on his mind, though
it might cost him some trouble.   Good Mart, therefore, after
the first show of mystery, had no further questions put to him,
or we are by no means sure that he would have refrained from
disclosing what, as it was, he had quite sufficient difficulty in
keeping to himself.   Meanwhile he was very busy and much
absent, going about the estate with the young Erra, who seemed
as if he could not be a day without him.

One afternoon at length he came rattling up to the door at
Sellenküll with his cart, jumped out, and strode over his own
threshold with more than usual alacrity.   Anno was sitting
spinning with Juhann at her side.

" Well! Anno," said he, " what say you to removing to
Uxnorm ?"

Anno looked up.   She did not mind what he said with such a
happy face as that.   And before she could answer, Mart had lifted
up Juhann with one hand, and the spinning-wheel with the
other, and had carried them out and put them into the cart.
Then he came back—bustled about Anno's little valuables in the
most extraordinary manner—stowed them all away in the cart—
threw in sheep-skins, and woollen coats, and Anno's best caps,
helter-skelter, with very little ceremony—told her she was of no
use, as she stood looking on in amazement—and finally lifted her
into the spare corner of the vehicle with as much gallantry as if
he had still been her bridegroom.   Then he called Karria Pois,
who, like his mistress, seemed much as if he did not care where
he went, so long as Mart was of the party, and set off walking by
the horse's side.

They took the road to Essmeggi—went past the great house,
now all whitewashing and putting to rights for the Baron's residence, and soon came in sight of the *Disponent's* cottage.

" A pretty house," said Mart, with his eyes sparkling.

" *Vegga illos* "—very pretty—said Anno.

In truth it looked prettier than ever; for the trees were so green, and the house had been fresh coloured like the Baron's own, and the garden seemed to have been put in order, and all around was swept clean.   Mart drove right up to it.

" You said you'd let me drive you here Anno, do you remember?"

" Yes, Mart—when you were *Disponent.*"

" I am, my *Einokenne,*" said her husband, and kissed her as he lifted her out.

We must pass over Anno's surprise ; for now Mart's was suddenly excited : he knew that the house had been thoroughly cleaned and repaired by his master's orders ; but now he found that during his few hours' absence it had been completely stocked with every household article that befitted their present condition.   There was good plain furniture, chairs and tables, and a little bed for Juhann, and provisions of all sorts, tubs full and bottles full ; and, above all, there was, what is the highest aim of a Livonian peasant's ambition, a tall clock ticking between the two windows.   Anno and Mart went about from one thing to another like two children, each looking at what the other had discovered, and both showing it to Juhann, who at length laughed and clapped his hands like a real child ; while Karria Pois knocked his great tail in a frenzy of wagging against every piece of furniture, and was considerably in the way.

They were still in the first bewilderment of their admiration, when steps were heard, and the young *Erra*, accompanied by the pastor, entered the house.   Mart set forward one of his new chairs, and Anno another ; and then they kissed their guest's hands ; but neither of them could say a word.

" Well, Mart," said the pastor, " I hope you have given Anno a warm welcome."

" You have got all your furniture about you, I see," said the Baron.

" Oh! the *Erra* is too good," said Mart.

" The *Erra* is too good," murmured Anno.

" No, Mart ; it is all your own goodness," said his master ; " you took care of my affairs when I was away, and now it is my turn to take care of yours."

" They deserve all you can do for them," said the pastor,

seriously. "They are an excellent couple, and the blessing of God, as well as the good will of man, is upon them. May they long enjoy both." Then seeing that Anno's eyes were brimful, he added—

"But Anno! have you nothing to give us for a welcome? Come, I think I know more about your new housekeeping than you do yourself;" and the pastor opened a little cupboard they had not yet observed, where stood a bottle of fine *Schälken*, with some rolls of white bread, and a few plates and glasses—things Anno had never possessed before. Then the two gentlemen drank to the health of the new *Disponent* and his wife, and with a further exchange of good wishes left them.

But the pleasures of this day was not yet over. There was one yet to come, which went nearer to Mart's heart than all the pastor and the *Erra* had said and done—good as that had been. For a party of his fellow-peasants came up, and with honest hearty words wished him joy; and told him that his being made *Disponent* was a greater joy to the parish even than the return of the *Erra*, for they did not know what he might turn out, but Mart they knew and could trust.

And then a few of the number took him aside, and told him that others might thank him, and even repay him for all the help and comfort he had afforded them that winter, but that they alone were indebted to him for what nothing could repay; for to him they owed the blessing of being able to look their fellow-creatures in the face, without the sin of murder upon their heads.

Then Mart went and opened one of his new bottles, and Anno set bread and milk and fish before them, and they made them eat and drink, and sent them away with gay hearts.

"This is like another wedding-day, Mart," said Anno, "only better."

"Yes," said her husband, "it is a happy day; would that some who are now gone had lived to see it! But God does all for the best."

THE WOLVES.*

THERE is a kind of savage luxury, however gorgeous and costly, which perfectly assimilates with savage life, and where the eye may pass at one glance from the pampered inmate of the palace to the wild beast in the woods, without any sense of inconsistency to the mind. This may be remarked, more or less, with all oriental nations. The Indian prince is in keeping with the tiger in the jungle, the Russian noble with the bear in his forests. But it is a different and very strange sensation·to find yourself in a country where inward and outward life are at variance ; where the social habits of the one by no means prepare you for the rude elements of the other ; where nature is wild, and man tame. This is conspicuously the case in the north-western part of Russia, where a German colony, although lords of the soil for hundreds of years, are still as foreign to it as they were at first ; having originally brought a weak offset of civilised life into a country for which only the lineal descendants of the savage were fitted, and having since then rather vegetated upon the gradually impoverishing elements they transplanted with them, than taken root in the gradually improving soil around them. Life, therefore, in this part of the world passes with a monotony and security which reminds you of what, in point of fact, it really is, viz. a remote and provincial state of German society of the present day. Both the inclinations and occupations of the colonists confine them to a narrow range of activity and idea. The country is too wild, the population too scattered, the distances too great, the impediments, both of soil and season, too many for them to become acquainted with the secrets of the wild nature around them ; or rather, not without a trouble which no one is sufficiently interested to overcome. They

* This story is reprinted, with permission, from 'Fraser's Magazine,' where it first appeared.

travel much, from place to place, upon roads bad enough, it is true, but always beaten ; they have no pursuit but mere business or mere pleasure, and no interest except in what promotes the one or the other ; and, in short, know as little of what goes on in the huts of the native peasantry, or in the forest and morass haunts of the native animals, as if they were strangers in the land, instead of its proprietors. It is, therefore, as we before remarked, a strange and most unpleasant feeling, while spending your days in a state of society which partakes of the security and ease of the present day, to be suddenly reminded by some accidental circumstance of a state of nature which recalls the danger and adventure of centuries back.

It was early in the spring, after a long and very severe winter, when the earth was just sufficiently softened to admit its stock of summer flowers, though not sufficiently warmed to vivify them, that the garden belonging to a country-house situated in this part of Russia had become the scene of great activity. Hundreds of leafless plants and shrubs, which has passed their winter in the darkness and warmth of the house-cellar, were now brought out to resume their short summer station, and lay strewed about in various groups, roughly showing the shape of the bed or border they were to occupy. The balmy air had also summoned forth the lovely mistress of the mansion, a delicate flower, more unsuited to this wintry land even than those which lay around her, who went from one plant to another, recognising in the leafless twigs the beautiful flowers which had been, or were to be, and shifting and reshifting their places on the fresh bare earth till they assumed that position which her taste or fancy approved—just as a fine London or Paris lady may be seen in a jeweller's shop shifting her loose diamonds, upon a ground of purple velvet, into the order in which they are to be finally set. A younger lady was with her—a cousin by birth and a companion by choice—who had recently joined her, after a long separation, in a home foreign to each. Her two children were there also, beautiful and happy creatures ; the elder one glad to be of use, the younger one delighted to think herself so ; while Lion, an enormous dog, the living image, in size, colour, and gentleness, of Vandyke's splendid mastiff in his picture of the children of Charles I., lazily followed their steps, putting up his huge head whenever a child stooped hers, and laying himself invariably down exactly where a flower was to be planted.

After spending some time in this occupation, and having at length marked out the summer-garden to their satisfaction, the party turned their steps towards the house, where some beds, close under the windows, had been planted the preceding evening.

" Lion, Lion !" exclaimed the eldest child, " you should know better than to come across the fresh-raked beds," showing us a tract of large, clumsy footmarks, which had gone directly over it. " Yes, look at the mischief you have done, old dog, and be ashamed of yourself ; but keep off now ! keep off !" for Lion was pressing forward with all his weight, snuffing at the prints with quick-moving nostrils. The lady stooped eagerly over the animal.

" These are no dog's footprints," she said ; and then, pointing to more distant traces farther on, " No, no. Oh, this is horrible ! And so fresh too. A *wolf* has been here !"

She was right ; the footmarks were very different from a dog's —larger and coarser even than the largest dog's, longer in shape, and with a deeper indentation of the ball of the foot. It was truly a painful and a fearful feeling to look at that flower-bed, on which the hand of man had been so recently employed, now tracked over by the feet of one of the most savage animals that exists ; and the lady drew back shuddering. And Louisa, for that was the cousin's name, shuddered too, if not with so real a sense of fear, yet with a much more unlimited impression of terror. She was a stranger as much to the idea as to the sight, and, as she looked up at the window just above—her own bedroom window —with its peaceful white curtains and swallow's nest at the corner, and remembered that she had been sleeping within while the wild beast was trampling beneath, she felt as if she should never rest easily there again. As for the children, they both looked terrified at first, chiefly because their elders did, and then each acted according to the character within her—Olga, the elder, holding quietly by her mother's hand, and afraid even to look at the footprints, though approaching them docilely when she was bidden ; while little Miss Constance, unscrewing her rosy face from its momentary alarm, trotted with great glee over the fresh-raked bed, delighted to make the most of a privilege usually forbidden her, and discovered new wolf's steps in all directions as fast as Lion made them.

They now called some of the workmen, who instantly confirmed their verdict.

"This is an old wolf, *Prauer*," said a rough, long-haired, shrewd-looking old peasant, scrutinising the tracts with Indian-like closeness and sagacity—"this is an old wolf, he walked so heavily; and here's a wound he has got to this paw, who knows when, from some other wolf, or maybe from Lion,—I dare say they are acquainted," pointing out to the party a slight irregularity in the print of one of the hind feet, as if from a distorted claw. He was here the beginning of the morning, that I can see."

"But where was Lion?" said the lady, eagerly.

"I went to the mill, *Prauer*, at sunrise, and took Lion with me, and by the time we got back the beast must have been off. I saw the old dog snuffing about, but the heavy dew would stop any scent. The wolves are hungry now, the waters have driven them up together, and the cattle are not let out yet. He is not far off, either; we must keep a sharp look-out. An old wolf like this will prowl about for days together round the same place, till he picks up something."

"Heavens! how dreadful! Constance, come back this moment," said the young mother, with an expression of anxiety which would have touched the roughest heart. "Who knows where the creature may be now?"

"Never fear, *Prauer*; he's off to the woods by this time—plenty of his footmarks to be found there, I warrant," pointing to a low, dismal-looking tract of brushwood, which formed the frontier to an immense morass, about a werst off. "Never fear; old Pertel and old Lion will take care of the little *Preilns*. *Polle üchtige!* nothing at all, not a hair on their heads shall be hurt, bless them!"

"Yes, yes, good Pertel," said the lady, with a nod and a smile, to the rough creature, "I know that. But under our very windows!—I never knew them come so near before."

"*Dreist wie ein wolf*—bold as a wolf," said the phlegmatic head-gardener, a German; "that's an old proverb."

They now returned to the house with minds ready to take alarm at any sight or sound. The cousin knew not how much there was or was not to fear; and, though the lady did, the voice of her maternal anxiety amply made up for all the silence of her imagination. The children, of course, were not slow in catching the infection; and, what with fear and what with fun, there was no end to the wolves that were seen in the course of the next four-and-twenty hours. Any and every object served their turn: sheep, foals, and calves; old men and old women; stunted trees in the distance, and round grey stones near; not to mention innumerable articles of furniture in various corners of the house— all stood for wolves; not only successively, but over and over again. Lion, however, was the greatest bugbear of all, and the good old dog could not push open the door, and come lazily in, with all his claws rattling on the smooth *parquête* floor, without setting the children screaming, and startling the two ladies much more than they liked to confess.

But this state of things was too inconvenient to last. A succession of false alarms is the surest cure for false fears; and, to quote the fable for once in its literal sense, they were weary of hearing "Wolf!" called. Nevertheless, they did not undertake long walks without protection, and never at all in the direction of the morass; the children were not allowed to wander a step alone; doors and windows, which otherwise, at this time of the year, are very much left to please themselves by night as well as by day, were now every evening punctiliously closed; and one door especially, next Louisa's bedroom, at the end of a long corridor, which communicated with an unfinished addition to the house then in progress, was always eyed with great distrust. It had no means of shutting whatsoever. Nightly a bar was talked of, and daily forgotten; but "*Dreist wie ein wolf!*" sounded in Louisa's ears, and she pushed a heavy box firmly against it.

Several days passed away, and the episode of the wolf's footprints was almost forgotten, when suddenly a scream and a shout were heard from a kind of baking-house within view of the windows. Lion started up from the cool drawing-room floor, where he lay stretched at full-length, and leaped out of the open window. Workmen from the new building rushed across the lawn, each with such implements in their hands as they had been working with; and out of the baking-house, followed by a lad, sprung an immense wolf. At first, he bounded heavily away, and was evidently making for the wood; but Lion came close upon him, overtook him in a few seconds, and attacked him with fury. The wolf turned, and a struggle began. For awhile the brave dog was alone; each alternately seemed to hang with deadly gripe upon the other, and yells, and snorts, and sharp howls filled the air. But now the foremost of the pursuers reached the spot; dog and wolf were so rolled together, that at first he stayed his blows; but soon a terrible stroke with the hatchet was given, —another, and another. The animal relinquished the dog, tried to turn upon the man, and soon lay dead at his feet.

Meanwhile, the ladies from the mansion were also hurrying forward, full of horror for the scene, and of anxiety for Lion, but unable, in the excitement of the moment, to keep back. There lay the animal, the ground ploughed up violently around it, a monstrous and terrific sight. Death had caught it in the most savage posture,—the claws all extended,—the hind feet drawn up, the fore ones stretched forward,—the head turned sharp round, and the enormous jaws, which seemed as if they would split the skull asunder, wide open. Nature could hardly show a more repulsive-looking creature—one which breathed more of the ferocity of the wild beast, or excited less of the humanity of man; and, as Louisa looked down at the lifeless carcass, all lean, starved, and time-worn, with ghastly gashes, where late every nerve had been strained in defence of that life which God had given it, entangling doubts came over her mind of the justice of that Power which could make an animal to be hated for that which His Will alone had appointed it to be. But, fortunately for her, she came from a land where, with all its faults, the stone of sophistry is not given for the bread of faith; quickly, therefore, came that antidote thought, which all who seek will find—the sole key to all we understand not in the moral world—leaving only a pardonable pity for a creature born to hunt and be hunted, ordained neither to give nor to find quarter, and to whom life had apparently been as hard as death had been cruel. Poor beast! It was a savage wolf all over; rough, coarse, clumsy, and strong; the hair, or rather bristles, dusky, wiry, and thin; and not one beauty about it, except, perhaps, those long, white, sharp teeth, which had drawn so much blood, and were now tinged with that of the fine old dog. Lion lay panting beside his dead enemy, the blood trickling down his throat, on which the wolf had fixed a gripe which life could not long have sustained.

The whole history was now heard from the lad. There had been baking going on that morning in the outhouse, and he went in to light his pipe. As he blew up the ashes he saw a great animal close beside him. In the dark he mistook it for Lion, and put out his hand; but it rose at once against him with an action not to be mistaken by a native of these climes; on which he screamed as loud as he could, for his breath stood still, the poor boy assured them, with fright; and the creature, taking alarm, rushed out of the door

" The *Prauer* may let the little ladies run about now," said old Pertel. "That's the same wolf that crossed the bed last Thursday; I know him by this left hind-foot;" and he held up a grim limb where an old wound had turned the claw aside. " He got this in some of his battles; many a foal yet unborn would have felt it this summer." And the old man stroked the dead animal with satisfaction.

They now all left the scene of battle, and refreshments were given to those who had assisted at it. Olga proposed giving the boy, who was still trembling with fright, a glass of sugar and water, this being what the ladies of this country invariably take when their nerves are shaken; but her mother suggested that a glass of brandy would be much more to his taste; and accordingly he received a dose, which not only restored the courage he had lost, but lent him a large temporary stock in addition. Lion, too, was well cared for, and immensely pitied. The wound on his throat, which was too close under his own long tongue to be reached by it, was washed with certain balsams with which this country abounds; after which, the old dog employed himself in slobbering over various rents and scratches in more accessible parts of his body, and finally went fast asleep, which the children hoped would do him much good, and, for about two minutes, spoke over him in whispers, and went round him on tiptoe.

Since the day of the footprints, the lady and her cousin had carefully refrained from any subject connected with wolves, or wild beasts in general; for the children's imaginations required to be studiously tranquillized, and even their own were quite lively enough without additional stimulus. But now nothing else was discussed; everything was *àpropos* of wolves; and some acquaintances from a distant part of the country coming in for the evening, the whole time was passed in telling wolf anecdotes.

The fact of the animal being discovered in the baking-house was soon explained; for it appeared that the wolf, like the bear, is excessively fond of bread, and that, after the smell of fresh blood, that of fresh baking is surest to attract him. A peasant woman, who had just drawn her hot rye-loaves out of the oven, quitted her cottage for a few minutes, leaving her two young children playing at the same bench on which the smoking bread was laid. Scarcely had she turned her back, when an enormous wolf sprang in, took no notice of the screaming children, but snatched a loaf from the bench. The mother, hearing screams, hastened back, and as she reached the door the wolf bounded out of it with the hot bread in his jaws. "I have heard the old woman often tell the tale," said the speaker; "and she invariably added, 'and so I lost my biggest loaf; but never was there a guest more welcome to it.'"

Another time, a kitchen-maid, whose office it is to bake the common rye bread, was carrying the hot loaves, towards night, across the court, when she met a large animal which she mistook in the dark for one of the huge cattle-dogs. But it rose upon her, and she felt the claws upon her bare arm, ready, at the next moment, to slit the skin, as is their wont, and rend her down. In her terror, she crammed a loaf into the creature's jaws, and he made off with the sop, perfectly content.

Upon the whole, it is very difficult to procure information about the wolf's habits, or even tidings of its depredations. The common peasant, who alone knows anything about the animal, is withheld by superstition from even mentioning the name of *wolf;* and if he mentions him at all, designates him only as the "old one," or the "grey one," or the "great dog;" feeling, as was also the case in parts of Great Britain with regard to the fairies, that to call these animals by their true name is a sure way to exasperate them. This caution may be chiefly attributed, how-

ever, to the popular and very ancient belief in the "*Wär Wolf;*"*
not a straightforward, open-mouthed, plain-spoken beast, against
which the cattle may plunge, and fight, and defend themselves as
best they may, and which either wounds or kills its prey in a fair
and ferocious way ; but that odious combination of human weakness and decrepitude, with demoniacal power and will, which all
nations who have believed in have most unjustly persecuted and
most naturally hated—in other words, a bad, miserable old
woman leagued body and soul with Satan, who, under the form
of a *Wär Wolf*, paralyses the cattle with her eye, and from whom
the slightest wound is death.   Be this as it may, the superior intelligence of the upper classes is to this day occasionally puzzled
to account for the fate of a fine young ox, who will be found in
the morning breathing hard, his hide bathed in foam, and with
every sign of fright and exhaustion, while, perhaps, only one
trifling wound will be discovered on the whole body, which
swells and inflames as if poison had been infused, the animal
generally dying before night.   Nor does the mystery end here;
for, on examining the body, the intestines will be found to be
torn as with the claws of a wolf, and the whole animal in a state
of inflammation, which sufficiently accounts for death.

This same superstition also favours the increase of this dreadful animal, for the peasant has a strong feeling against destroying
a wolf; says that, if you disturb them, they will disturb you,
and generally attributes the loss of his foal, or of foal and mother
together (a too frequent occurrence), to the plunder of a wolf's
nest by his less superstitious neighbour.   Nevertheless the destruction of their young is the only way in which an efficient
warfare with the wolf can be carried on, and the provincial government of this part of Russia wisely bestows a small reward in
money for every pair of wolves' ears that is brought to the magistrate of the district ; thus setting up one powerful passion in the
human breast against another.   But superstition has the best of

* " This mysterious and widely spread superstition—the ware wolf of
England, the *loup garrou* of France—was especially current in Germany,
where many tales of its terror still exist.   Two warlocks were executed in
the year 1810, at Liege, for having, under the form of ware wolves, killed
several children.   They had a boy of twelve years of age with them, who
completed the Satanic trio, and, under the form of a raven, consumed those
portions of the prey which the warlocks left."—Grimm's *Deutsche Sagen.*

it at present, and, perhaps, in the long run, is the better thing of the two.

The wolves make their nests usually deep in the morasses. a few sticks being dragged together in a small hollow, or under a juniper-bush, where the young wolves lie with great jaws, which open wide at the slightest noise, like the bill of a young bird, and equally disproportionate to their size. It is at this season that the wolves are the most rapacious and dauntless, defying danger, and facing daylight to provide prey for their young. In old times, if tradition is to be believed, the abduction of peasant children for the young wolves was a thing of no uncommon occurrence, so that the father of a former day had as little chance of rearing all his children as the farmer of the present his foals. But now, with the culture of the land, and the gradual increase of farming stock, a favourable change has taken place, and the recent introduction of sheep especially has proved a great accommodation to both parties. Nevertheless, the wail of a poor peasant mother for a missing child is still raised from time to time, though the widely scattered population, and the remote situation of single villages, on that account more exposed to such depredations, allow only the occasional echo of such distress to reach the ears of the upper classes. The peasant also is an uncommunicative being; the slave of one set of foreigners, the subject of another, and oppressed by both, he shuts up his mouth and his heart, and cares little to divulge the more sacred sorrows of his life to those who are the authors of almost every other.

The evening visitors, however, related a wonderful instance which had occurred under their own knowledge:—A peasant child, just able to trot alone, and as such left to trot just where it pleased, was carried off unperceived and unhurt by a she-wolf to her nest at some distance. The young wolves, however, had just consumed some larger and commoner prey, and knew when they had had enough; so they let the child lie among them, and saved it up for another day. The little creature remained thus through the night, when the old one quitting the nest again, and the young ones probably sleeping, it crawled gradually away, as unintentional of escape as it had been unconscious of danger, and at length reached the fence of a remote field, where it was picked up by a labourer and brought to the house of the narrator. But the innocent child had suffered terribly, and bore upon its tender body such marks of the wolf's den as would, so long as it lived, sufficiently attest an otherwise almost incredible fact. The young wolves had forborne to devour their prey, but they had *tasted* it ! The skin of the forehead was licked raw ; all the fingers were more or less injured, but two of them were sucked and mumbled completely off!

This tale was now followed by another more tragic and equally true, having taken place only the summer before upon a neighbouring estate, so that the lady of the house, her beautiful brow contracted, and her voice lowered, related it herself to the party. A woman, whose husband, being a *Junker*, or something less obnoxious than a *Disponent*, lived in a more comfortable way than the usual run of peasants, though still classing as a peasant, was washing one day before the door of her house, with her only child, a little girl of four years old, playing about close by. Her cottage stood in a lonely part of the estate, forming almost an island in the midst of low, boggy ground. She had her head down in the wash-tub, and, hot and weary, was bending all her efforts to complete her task, when a fearful cry made her turn, and there was the child, clutched by one shoulder, in the jaws of a great she-wolf, the other arm extended to her. The woman was so close that she grasped a bit of the child's little petticoat in her hand, and with the other hand, screaming frantically, beat the wolf with all her force to make it let go its hold. But those relentless jaws stirred not for the cries of a mother—that gaunt form cared not for the blows of a woman. The animal set off at full speed with the child, dragging the mother along, who clung with desperation to her grasp. Thus they continued for two or three dreadful minutes, the woman only just able to hold on. Soon the wolf turned into some low, uneven ground, and the woman fell over the jagged trunk of a tree, tearing in her fall the piece of petticoat, which now only remained in her hand. The child hitherto had been aware of its mother's presence, and, so long as she clung, had not uttered a scream ; but now the little victim felt itself deserted, and its screams resounded through the wood. The poor woman rose in a moment, and followed over stock and stone, tearing herself pitiably as she went, yet

K 2

knowing it not; but the wolf increased in speed, the bushes grew thicker, the ground heavier, and soon the screams of the child became her only guide. Still she dashed on, frantic with distress, picked up a little shoe which the closing bushes had rubbed off, saw traces of the child's hair and clothes on the low, jagged boughs, which crossed the way; but, oh! the screams grew fainter, then louder, and then ceased altogether!

"The poor mother saw more on her way, but I can't tell what that was," said the lady, her voice choked with horror, and her fair face streaming with tears. Her hearers did not press to know, for they were chilled enough already. "And only think," she continued, "of the wretchedness of the poor afflicted creature, when her husband returned at night and asked for the child. She told me that she placed the piece of petticoat and the little shoe before him, but how she told him their great misery God only knows! she has no recollection. And now you don't wonder," she added, "that I shuddered at seeing those footprints;" and she shuddered again. "Sometimes I am in terror when my children are longer out of my sight than usual, and fancy every person that approaches me is charged with some dreadful announcement; but God avert this! mistrust is wrong."

With these words the circle broke up. The long *droshky,* like a *chaiselongue* put upon wheels, came to the door, and the guests drove off. It was one of those exquisite nights peculiar to these climes, which the French aptly term *des nuits blanches,*—a night, light without moon, a day shaded without clouds,—the last glow of the evening and the first grey of morning melted together; a period when all the luminaries of the heavens seem to rest their beams without withdrawing them. The cousins stood at the door, hand in hand, gazing in the direction which their guests had taken; and a looker-on might have imagined they were envying them that calm, cool drive. But they envied them not; they honoured all that was good in this strange land, and prized all who were good to them; but a sense of solitude hung heavy upon them in the society of others, which only the solitude of their own could dispel. They had much, also, to say to one another, which a native of these climes could not comprehend, or would not like. Not that they said aught that was strange, or wrong, or unkind; but they spoke as they thought, and they thought unlike all the world around them. So they lingered beneath that beautiful light, talking calmly of what was peculiar in their lot, yet not complaining of the evil, but rather extracting the good; and they spoke, too, as those speak who have no time to lose, but rather much to recover, plainly, earnestly, and touchingly, because so truly; each seeking to give knowledge of her own mind, and comfort to that of her companion. And from that which concerned their own hearts individually they soon passed on to that which concerns every heart that beats; and thoughts came which all have heard, but not all have listened to—thoughts which are locked to some, checked to others, and not even breathed freely to the most kindred spirit, except at those moments, few and fleeting, which favour their utterance and suit their sacredness. They discoursed on the wonderful economy of happiness in a world full of woe; how, the fewer the joys, the higher the enjoyment, till the last and highest of all, true peace of mind, is found to contain every other. And then they spoke of the blessing of sorrow, and of the mystery of sin, and turning to her companion that angel's face, more angelic still in the soft light, and with a transition of expression peculiar to herself, the lady added,—

" And sin brought the wolves too, dear one !"

" True, true," said Louisa; " I thought of that when the poor beast lay dead at our feet to-day."

And so they turned and went into the house.

They now took their usual last look at the children, who slept in opposite cots in the same room. Each lay the sleeping effigy of her waking self. The eldest, composed, cool, and orderly; with pale cheek and smooth hair; the limbs straight, the head gently bent, the bed-clothes lying unruffled upon the regularly heaving chest; all that was beautiful, gentle, and meek; looking as if stretched out for a monumental effigy. On the other side, defying all order and bursting all bounds, was the little Constance, flushed, tumbled, and awry; the round arms tossed up, the rosy face flung back, the bed-clothes pushed off, the pillow flung out, the nightcap one way, the hair another; all that was disorderly and most lovely by night—all that was unruly and most winning by day.

"Come, my lovely one, mamma will set all to rights!" And, with a few magical movements, which the young mother's hand best knows, the head was raised up, the limbs smoothed down, the little form adjusted into a fresh position, and, with sighs and smiles, and a few murmuring sounds, the blooming creature was fast asleep again.

"Only think, that poor woman's child was the age of Constance!"

"Don't think of it," said Louisa, "it will haunt your sleep;" and she led her cousin to her room through the children's, where they parted for the night.

"You need not shut the children's door, nor any as you go along; the house is oppressively warm, and Constance is hot."

Louisa came through two halls and down the corridor, looked at the door into the new building, and remembered that the bar had again been forgotten; pushed the box again up, and then went into her own room and shut the door.

The night, as we have described, was one of those which seem too good to be passed in sleep. Louisa was sad and serious, and all without and within tempted her to watch. But so long as the heaviness of the heart can yield to that of the head, there is not much that is amiss in either. By the time, therefore, that she had fully resolved to lie awake, recalling old griefs and conjuring up new, past and future, with their cares and fears, had vanished away, and of the present she knew as little as the children she had left in their cots.

How long this lasted she knew not, some hours it seemed, when she was roused by a sound in the adjoining unfinished building. At first the drowsy senses paid little attention, and dozed on; but again she was roused, louder and louder, and, starting up, she shook off sleep, flew out of bed, and, opening the door, looked into the dark passage. To her astonishment the door into the new building was half open; she advanced to shut it, when again a noise made her turn her head in the opposite direction; and there—oh, Heavens! the poor girl's blood froze in her veins—there, stealing down the passage, its back towards her, was—a wolf! An exclamation of horror which burst from her lips disturbed the animal; it turned, and the light from the half-open door shone on its green eyes and white

teeth as it sprang upon her. With one convulsive bound Louisa
cleared the threshold, dashed her door to, locked it, barred it,
flung a chair against it, and, this done, stood in a state of agony
for which no words exist. She seemed to see all in a moment;
herself safe, but those children!—those children! not a door
closed between them and those dreadful jaws! She was stupified with terror, and a strange, dinning sound, like her heart's
own throbbing, filled her ears, and shut out every other sense.
" *Dreist wie ein Wolf!—Dreist wie ein Wolf!*" she repeated,
mechanically; and then, forcing herself from the fainting,
trance-like feeling that oppressed her, she thought for one moment that she would follow the wild beast. Her hand was on
the lock, but she looked round for some weapon of defence.
There was not a thing she could use,—not a stanchion to the
window, not a rod to the bed. Then she listened at the door,
and distinctly heard the trampling claws on the boards. The
animal was still close to her door, and there was time, if she
could keep her senses together, to consider some means of help.
Oh, if she could but have stopped that dinning sound in her ears !
but it came again, beating louder and louder, and perfectly
paralysed her. The effort to open the window restored her.
How she got out she knew not, but there she was on the damp
ground, alone in the open garden. And now there was no time
to be lost; she had to get round the end of the house, which
was half closed up with bushes, half blocked up with building
materials, stones, and timber. But the night had grown darker;
she could not see the path ; she knew that she was losing time,
and yet that all depended on her haste ; she felt fevered with impatience, yet torpid with terror. At length she disengaged herself from the broken, uneven ground, and struggled forward.
There were the windows of the children's and her cousin's rooms ;
she had fancied that she could reach and open them with her hands,
and call to those within ; but how confused was her head ! they
belonged to a later part of the house, and were much higher than
her own. She called and called, but her voice failed, and no
one answered ; she stooped for a stone or something to throw up,
but only soft grass or moist leaves came into her hand. Suddenly a scream was heard, it was Constance's voice,—scream
over scream. Frantic with terror, Louisa now dashed to another

part of the house where the servants slept. As she reached it, a figure came towards her. Thank Heaven, it was old Pertel! But those screams ;—they reached her louder and louder! She could only ejaculate, " *Weiche Preilns !—Weiche Preilns !*"— " The little ladies—the little ladies !" But he seemed neither to heed her words nor the dreadful sounds that impelled them, and took her hand, in peasant fashion, to kiss it. " *Weiche Preilns !—Weiche Preilns !*" she reiterated; but again he took her hand. She struggled, but he held it firm. She looked down, and there was the fairest, softest hand locked round hers ; she looked up, and there was the sweetest, gentlest face bent laughing over her.

" I must say, darling, you speak better Esthnish in your sleep than you do when you are awake. What has made you sleep so late ? Olga has been knocking twice at your door,—she would not come in unbidden for the world,—and Constance has been screaming, in one of her fits of play, till the whole house heard her. And when I came at last, and took your hand to waken you, you only knocked it aside, and ejaculated ' *Weiche Preilns !*' with such a pitiable expression, that I woke you with my laughing. How sound you have slept !"

" Slept !" said Louisa, " indeed I have,—such a sleep as I never wish for again ! But I see it all ; the wolf of yesterday— Olga's knocking—Constance's screaming—your hand !" And she related her dream.

The cousins laughed together, but also thanked God together that such scenes only exist in dreams. For wolves neither jump up to windows, nor open doors, nor walk up and down corridors. Nevertheless, a bar was put on to that door before night.

THE JEWESS:

A TALE FROM THE SHORES OF THE BALTIC.

UPON the eastern shores of the Gulf of Finland, at the distance of about a hundred wersts from the ancient city of Narva, lies an estate called Kunda, equally rich in the beauties of nature and the relics of antiquity. Here vegetation of a more varied and luxuriant character is found than usually occurs in this northern latitude ; the oak and the beech, intermingled with rich plots of grass, grow at the very edge of the waves, and there being no tides in the Baltic, the rights of boundary are very peacefully kept. For about half a werst in breadth the shore continues a flat luxuriant strip, when it suddenly rises in three successive cliffs, each above a hundred feet high, and placed about the same half-werst one behind the other, like huge steps leading to the table-land above. In some places the rocks are completely hidden from the view by a thick fence of trees which take root at their base ;—the vigorous firs shooting far above their rounder, deciduous brethren, and climbing with their clean-cut, ladder-like branches, like a spiral staircase round a slender column, in tapering lines up to the summit of the cliff;—while each flat landing-place gives footing to another sturdy forest, and between every bold trunk which skirts the edge lies enframed the same never-tiring picture of sea and sky and luxuriant foreground. Such is the character of two of these cliffs ; at the third the rocks rise less abruptly, and, except the grass and wild flowers which creep in horizontal lines between the division of the strata, and the wild strawberries and low shrubs which nestle in their recesses, including even a few sprays of English white-thorn—a rare colonist in this clime,—not an object breaks their rugged sides.

This last cliff surmounted, the view now opens over a vast

bleak plain, flat as the Gulf itself, and so devoid of all natural objects, that it seems as if the winds from the Baltic had compromised matters with the smiling valley below, by sweeping all signs of fertility from the plain above. Here, on the very edge of the topmost cliff, commanding a panoramic view, unmatched on the one hand for beauty, and on both for extent, and exposed to every blast that blows beneath heaven, the caprice or boldness of an architect has placed a large mansion, standing like a lonely sentinel's box at the edge of a fortress, and visible in a square mass for miles around. Forwarder in the plain lie a few scattered buildings, and upon the same line with the house itself may be seen an old mill, now a ruin, but sacred from further demolition from the circumstance of its forming, as well as the mansion, a land-mark for navigation. Other and more interesting relics of antiquity are discernible from this height, for deeper in the country may be seen the bold ruins of the Castle of Wesenberg, and beneath the cliffs, on a tongue of land jutting into the sea, stands the ancient pile of the Tolsburg.

But to return to the house. To those who approach it from the plain for the first time, it appears no less the emblem than the abode of utter desolation ; and as the land lies in a gentle, almost imperceptible slope up to its very threshold, not a glimpse of the valley beneath or sea beyond is visible till the traveller has entered its walls. Such being the case, he generally finds himself stationed at a window overlooking the full magnificence of the scene, before he is even aware of its existence ; while his astonished gaze follows the receding masses of forest which hang round each depression of the cliff,—lingers along the slender line of shore studded with solitary groups of trees and huge masses of boulder stones, and thence launches freely on a wide expanse of waters, broken only by the bold outline of the mountainous island of Hochland resting upon the horizon.

On this coast, so dreary above and so smiling beneath, scenes of danger and adventure, arising from a system of illicit traffic, had often been witnessed ; for, far removed from the widely scattered towns of their own country, where a selfish Russian policy only offers for sale the wretched articles of its own inland manufactures, and those at exorbitant prices, the inhabitants of this wild region are doubly induced to welcome across the Finlanders from the opposite shores, whose own comparatively unrestricted commerce enables them to offer the various products of foreign growth or excellence at a moderate price. Moreover, the Finlanders are content to forego money and take goods in exchange, a mode of payment particularly convenient in this part of the world; and thus the sledge or boat, which comes freighted with coffee, sugar, English cottons, and other tempting articles, generally returns laden with a cargo of corn or brandy. Owing to the extent to which this system of traffic, equally illegal on both sides, was carried on, the vigilance of government had been attracted, and a species of preventive guard, called *Strandreiters*, consisting of a body of mounted Cossacks, was established along the coast; their head-quarters being about four wersts, nearly as many miles, from the mansion we have described. These individuals were hated as a matter of course, and cheated by the same rule; while, for some time, the traffic only seemed to acquire fresh zest and activity from the difficulties which attended it. Altogether the peasants here are a more manly race than are usually met with in this part of Russia. This is owing to their wild locality; to their frequent intercourse with the islanders of the Baltic, all, as well as the Finlanders, hardy and independent races; and to their favourite pursuit of seal-hunting and other nautical occupations, which vary their more peaceful agricultural labours.

Towards the period, however, when our story opens, owing to the appointment of a new subaltern officer to this post, whose character for courage and cruelty was noted, and who had put the latter beyond all question by taking the law of punishment, in some cases, most barbarously into his own hands, the ardour for smuggling had much abated. At the same time, it must be owned that the shifting state of the Baltic,—as perfidious in its frozen as in its liquid form,—owing to a succession of high and suddenly changing winds, not a little contributed to the maintenance of order on the coast. It was not, indeed, till so late as the month of March that the ice-masses became knit together, and that the *Strandreiters* assumed a more vigilant look-out.

But we must again return to the far-seen house upon the cliff, where our narrative rightly begins. In one of the many apartments of the lower story, which usually in houses of this rank is entirely appropriated to the numerous retinue of servants, there was gathered together a most picturesque group. At a long table, which divided the room lengthwise, and wrapped in the tanned sheep-skin, which covers alike the Russian, the Finlander, and the inhabitant of the Baltic provinces, stood a man with a short, black, curling beard, and quick piercing glance, busily engaged in unpacking and displaying the various contents of a huge pack; while around him, with every variety of active and passive curiosity expressed in their countenances, were congregated a group of female household servants. The younger women wore their hair—generally most profuse in quantity—carefully braided, and disposed around the head, not unlike a picture by Raphael; while the matrons of the party were distinguished by high helmet-shaped caps of every colour, decorated behind with long flowing ribbons. Some of these neat-handed Phillises were already employed in a close examination of the folds of *Sitze*, or print, or rolls of soft woollen material, which the pedlar was unwrapping, while others, less venturesome, stood leaning with their elbows on the table, in perfect wonderment of the treasures, or whispered some joke at their bolder companions' expense, which, though it elicited much mirth at the time, might not perhaps appear quite so witty if translated here. On the other side of the room, in irregular groups, sat as many as twelve or fourteen spinners, all enrobed in gay striped petticoats of native manufacture, with coarse cloth jackets, short-waisted, and of a dull grey or blue colour, though a few of the number, tacitly confessing they were too hot, a fact which this warmth-loving, northern people very rarely admit, had thrown off this upper garment, displaying thereby to view their coarse crimped shifts, all embroidered with more or less labour in coloured silks or studded with slender spangles. All of these spinning nymphs wore their long hair utterly uncurbed by cap, comb, or ribbon, in smooth, rope-like tresses on their shoulders and bosoms. It would seem, indeed, as if this national coiffure, worn among the lower peasantry by man and woman alike, had been adopted expressly to favour the national quality—for we will not call it virtue—of bashfulness; for not only do the women of all ages hang their heads in the presence of a superior at an angle sufficiently acute for their pendent locks effectually to hide their blushing countenances, but even the male peasants themselves, in moments of particular embarrassment, by no means disdain to fall back upon the same ready protection. Occupying a considerable space at one end of the room was an immense stove, built of large slabs of brick, whose colours, varying through all the shades of red and brown, seemed emblematical of their temperature. At this a stout kitchen girl, attired much in the same costume as her spinning sisters, was busied alternately putting in and taking out the large dark rye-loaves, which hardly differed in appearance from the logs which fed the fire. On the same side was a door leading to a smaller apartment which communicated with the outer air, in the open portal of which stood a few sturdy peasants, with their sandalled feet, long coats girded at the waist, and flowing locks; while behind them were seen a couple more engaged in sharpening their pikes preparatory to a seal-hunt.

Such were the many tenants of this room. But one yet remains to be mentioned, and one whose appearance, to gentle eyes, was more interesting than that of all the rest. On a rough chair close to the door we have described, and thrown into deep light and shade by a high window, sat a youthful female figure; so youthful, indeed, that it seemed impossible that the sleeping child which hung in a kind of sling before her should be her own. But, on looking in her face, a certain languid expression, which bespoke the cares of the matron and mother, though clothed in the round contours of the tenderest girlish youth, was distinctly visible. Her beauty was great,—in truth, too great to be fully appreciated by the company in which she now sat; for she was pale as marble, her features were delicate and regular, and her large violet-blue eyes gazed upon the spectator with an unconscious pathos, as if lamenting the little sympathy they found. Her dress was poor,—even tattered; an old *Kasavoika* or half-cloak, lined with fur, hung negligently upon her, and barely covered her small round arms, and nothing betrayed her real origin except her head, which was bound in a turban of indubitable Hebrew form. This also told her history; for in the mixture of loftiness and gentleness which her countenance expressed, seemed equally united the sense of her people's wrongs and their habits of passive endurance. She sat with an air of perfect unconcern, now looking listlessly at the busy party, or at the strapping damsel at the oven, who, with her red face and fat arms, and fragrant steaming load, looked the very personification of vulgar plenty.

" You have a large batch there, *Matuschka*," said the young stranger, at length breaking silence, and seemingly indifferent how she began the conversation.

" No more than we shall want," answered the red-faced scullion; " we have none to spare for Jews."

" If you keep your bread till I ask for it, it will be stale," was the laconic reply. And here, doubtless, the Christian damsel would have found an equally charitable retort, had not all further conversation been arrested by the entrance of another individual.

This was no less a personage than the lady of the house; summoned to view those wares of which she alone was likely to become a purchaser. At sight of her the conclave round the pedlar broke up; each smiling maid-servant suddenly remembered that, whilst she was examining coloured cottons and gay ribbons, her household labours, in all probability, did not progress, and now moved off, each her own way, with an air as if she were only just come, and had never intended to stop. The lolling peasants at the door retreated with precipitation; the spinners' heads sunk on their bosoms; and the spinning-wheels, which had been describing most languid circles, now whirled with great energy. None, in short, remained save the lady's own maid,—a Russian nymph of unquestionable national physiognomy,—who thought herself privileged to do what her mistress did, and the housekeeper, a stately dame with an erect cap, who, detecting one of the spinning-girls peeping at the lady through a chink in her wall of hair, suddenly broke out into such tones of reprimand as implied that her authority had never relaxed. But it was not less the individual than the station which gave rise to all this demonstration of respect; for although the mistress wore on her whole aspect an air of the utmost Christian and feminine gentleness, yet there was something in her look and carriage which told, not of that equivocal quality, so misnamed, which springs from a helpless and negative character,—provoking minds of more power not seldom to demonstrations of a very opposite nature, and meeting rarely with more respect than it deserves,—but rather the acquired control over warm feelings often tried, and the submission of a lofty spirit to loftier convictions. Her eye was thoughtful, and her whole deportment serious; nevertheless, there was that lurking animation in her face which showed that a gleam of merriment or sparkle of sarcasm would still flash up from the suppressed fires within. She glanced round the room, and her eye rested on the figure of the Jewess, who, now quitting her listless posture, rose with the child in her arms at the lady's entrance. As their looks met, a spectator might have fancied some resemblance between them; both countenances were so pale and so beautiful, and both marked with an expression of experience beyond their years. But they might almost have exchanged their birthright; for the Christian lady's eye was full, dark, and of an Oriental languor, and her eyebrow slender and arched like Lot's daughter in Guido's picture; while the young Israelite's deep blue eye and tender brow might better have found its prototype among the high-born daughters of an island kingdom.

"*Seditez*"—be seated, said the lady, and the Jewess dropped to her former position.

"And whence do you come?"

"Across the Gulf, Sudārina,"* replied the pedlar himself, in a broken Russo-German.

"But you must have had a dangerous journey!"

"Dangerous! *Vasche Ciātelstvo* (your Grace), by no means; the track across the Baltic is now as level the whole way, excepting a few holes, as the centre of a frozen stream."

"Did you come, then, through the past night?" added the lady, looking with compassion at the young woman and child.

"Sudārina, no," said the pedlar with a little hesitation. "We landed late, and slept in an outhouse here," interposed the Jewess, pointing in the direction of the stables; and then, embarrassed perhaps at the avowal, and conscious of the lady's fixed gaze, a blush passed over her pale face, as tender and clear as the last reflection of light at sunset over the peak of the *Jungfrau*. The pedlar now, as if desirous to avoid further questioning, hurriedly pursued—

* Lady, or Signora.

" The Kaufmann Mendelssohn, from whom the Sudárina took the coffee and sugar and the beautiful English stuffs last year, has been waiting all this winter to send the Sudárina what she ordered, but the *bahn* (ice-track) has been so bad, I could not come before."

" I am more sorry you came at all. Did he not receive my message? I sent him word not to venture himself, or any one; the *Strandreiters* are so strict now, it is hard to escape them ; and the goods are not worthy of the peril."

" It is not fear that will keep your servant from waiting on the Sudárina ; though it is true the low price of the wares (and they are precious goods) is far from covering the expense of the transport," said the pedlar, beginning his speech in his Russian and ending it in his Hebrew nature. " I have a valuable cargo, —sugar double-refined,—coffee, the best, at seventy kopecks the pound ; the Sudárina can't buy it at Narva under two roubles,— and that bad. And *Sitze* for the little *Bárishnas'* holiday frocks. French silks and English shawls. The Sudárina will send me back with a light sledge, and Rose will ride the whole way."

" And is that your wife?" said the lady, who had evidently been much more occupied with the Jewess's countenance than with the pedlar's catalogue.

" Sudárina, I am his wife," said the young creature.

" But that is not your child; no, it cannot be,—you look but a child yourself."

" Matvei is my child," said the Jewess, with a glance of her liquid eye towards the sleeper, which superseded any other affirmative.

" Poor young creature," said the lady in a low tone, and in a language which none there understood ; and then addressing the pedlar, " How could you venture to bring your wife such a journey? Are you not afraid of injuring her health?"

The pedlar smiled at this question. " Rose is accustomed to it," he said; " she can sleep as well beneath the straw in the sledge as the Sudárina beneath her silken coverlet."

" I 'll be bound she has nothing better at home," said Axina, the Russian waiting-maid, who was already much deeper engrossed in the contents of the pack than her mistress, in a half-whisper to Tina, the stately housekeeper.

"Nay, Axina, girl, but he must be a bold man who could leave such a pretty young wife (if she be his wife) at home ; she is safest with him," replied Tina.

"Safe, indeed," retorted the Russian Grace; "it would be an odd taste that could fancy such a *jidskoe* face, and a bold heart that would venture near any of her race: before a Christian can say *Sdrāstite?** as the saying goes, they 'll pick your pockets."

"You are a fool, Axina," said her mistress, who happened to overhear her—the Russian equivalent to this being more customary, if not more polite; "her face is not so Jewish as your own, to say nothing of its being a trifle handsomer ; and as to picking pockets, one of your own Russians will outwit a Jew any day. Here, take my keys, and fetch bread and meat from the *schafferei*,† and white bread for the child. Do you hear? *Skorēe*, quick."

At this double insult on herself and her nation, followed up by a commission which by no means smoothed the matter, poor Axina's lips protruded beyond all bounds even of Tartar symmetry ; and this, with the slowest possible execution of orders, being the only means of expressing her injured dignity left to her, it is but just to add that she made the most of both before she finally quitted the room.

"What may be the price of this blue Navarino, pedlar?"—and then, without waiting or listening for the answer, "And what's your age, *Jevraica?*"‡ added the lady, who stood between the gay pile of goods and the poor tattered girl.

"Sudārina, I am sixteen summers old ;" for the Russians reckon by this brief season, though their neighbours, the Laplanders, compute by frosts.

"Sixteen summers !" repeated the lady with somewhat of horror ; "too young, too young. Why were you in such haste to begin the cares of life? they come soon enough of themselves. And your child?"

"Matvei can walk alone ; come, *Dūschinka*, show the *Bārina* how well you can stand," said Rose, putting a little misshapen bundle down, which first pitched on its head, then settled on to a

---

* How do you do?   † Store-room.   ‡ Hebrew.

more central part, and thence, being quickly jerked upright by its mother, began to show symptoms of tolerably lively limbs beneath.

"What a pretty child! Such beautiful eyes are too good for a boy; they were better bestowed on one of my little girls," said the lady, with a smile of encouragement.

"The Sudārina then is blessed with children?" said the Jewess, and a glance of maternal freemasonry passed between them, which would probably have been further amplified by words, when Axina entering with provisions, the lady resumed her examination of the pack.

The pedlar now displayed all his treasures, and for some time nothing was discussed but textures and patterns, roubles and kopecks; while Axina, at her mistress's elbow, cast looks of true Russian longing at a flaunty red chintz with yellow flowers, the most indubitable bit of internal manufacture the pack afforded, which she determined to bargain for at the very first pause, and beat down at every successive one.

"Then I may cut the Sudārina sixteen ells of the French Navarino; and how many of the checked print?"

"Eighteen ells, my good man."

"Surely the Sudārina will take the whole, exactly three and twenty; five ells more will just be a frock for one of the little Bārishnas. There 's no fear of its fading in the wash: I 'll pledge myself it will come out brighter every time, like the green leaves in summer after a shower of rain. Come, you shall have the last five ells ten kopecks cheaper."

"Very well, you may leave it; but what 's the price of this *Englische Leder?* (English leather, alias stay-jean) How beautiful it is! how different to what one gets here. Axina, feel here; this will be hard work for your fingers."

Axina lent a disparaging eye, for she was too good a patriot to praise foreign wares. But the Jew knew no distinction; all he had was first-rate.

"'Tis a choice article; I 'll sell it cheap: what says *Vasche Ciātelstvo* to six roubles the ell?" with a look at the same time as if he thought he might raise his price on the strength of her admiration, but rather doubting her concurrence.

"Six roubles an ell? Absurd! No English merchant would

ask above a fourth of that price, and you have paid no duty. Put it back again, Axina."

" Nay, Sudārina, I would rather be a loser than you; *Nu*, you shall have it for five roubles."

" More than twice its value; but I never bargain: if it were not English, I would not look at it twice."

" Well, the Sudārina may please to change her mind," said the Jew, smiling obsequiously; " will she look, meanwhile, at some beautiful *Calinchor*—genuine English; here 's the maker's name," pointing to a hieroglyphic of rather doubtful meaning at the fag end: "and English needles, too; I have plenty of English goods this time;" and as the first-named article was produced, the lady stooped her head, and gave it that peculiar rub between both hands with which discerning buyers of linen invariably begin, and then throwing down the loose-woven dusty goods:

" English calico! what trash! No English hands ever felt this cotton;—before now, at least," she added in a low tone. " And your needles? no better: do you call these English? Pray don't fill your sledge with such wares when you cross again: I could supply you with either better."

" The Sudārina appears to know all about English wares," continued the pedlar, still smiling imperturbably; " has the Sudārina ever been in England?"

" I never left it till I came here," was the slow and serious answer.

" *Mōschno li!* Is it possible! *Chudēznoi!* wonderful! *Bōje mōi!* my God! Then the Sudārina was an Englishwoman?"

" *Was* an Englishwoman! I *am* an Englishwoman as much as you are a—Russian (she was going to say "a Jew"), and shall never be otherwise."

These last few sentences had roused the Jewess from her customary apathy, and hastily rising, she exclaimed, "How could the Bārina leave her own land? To be sure, Russia is a pleasant country, and England, they say, is but a poor place to live in; but each one loves their own. Has the Bārina then no *Pāpinka* or *Māminka?*"

" Yes," said the lady, smiling mournfully at Rose's sudden ebullition; " yes, my mother, God bless her, is alive, but I have not seen her for many long years."

" *Bŏje mŏi!* how could you leave her?"

" Nay, Rose, you have no right to question me. I did like
yourself, I married young, and now I am older I must be wise
enough to make the best of it. Women must follow their husbands, you know; you Russians follow yours on a mournful
errand sometimes. And I am as happy as most are," she added,
with a sigh which somewhat qualified the assertion.

" *Nu,*—if the Bārina be but happy, that's enough. 'Tis true,
there's nothing like your own country and kinsfolk; but a good
husband is worth travelling after. And one husband, I dare
say, is as good as another," added Rose, with rather a novel
species of philosophy, which her own husband might not have
quite so readily approved. But the pedlar seemed fully to par-
take of the sympathising emotions which evidently swelled the
heart of his young wife, and looking at the beautiful lady with
his blandest expression, " Say no more about it; Sudārina shall
have her *Englische Leder* at four roubles; nay, I'll say three
roubles, eighty kopecks;" and there's no knowing how his abate-
ments might not have proceeded, when suddenly the light at the
window was obscured, and the lady's quick eye was the first to
recognise the figure of a horseman, who, pike in hand, and
mounted on a high saddle, overlooked the window which no
pedestrian figure could have reached, and stood gazing for a
second at the party through the dusky double panes. A quick
glance of fear spoke her anxiety as she hastily motioned the Jew
and his wife to a part of the apartment screened by the stove, and
then, quick as thought, threw the despised calico over the mul-
tifarious pack. Scarcely was this effected when one of the long-
haired peasants put his head round the door-stall and mysteriously
whispered, " The *Strandreiter,*"—a communication which was
immediately followed by a confusion of voices and trampling of
feet at the outer door.

" What shall I do? What shall I do?" said the Jew trembling
from head to foot, while Rose leant with her child against the
warm stove and exhibited no signs of fear.

" Keep quiet," said the lady, " and you will lose nothing."

" But my sledge! my sledge! it is at the door; and the good
black horse, and a *liesspfund* and a half of coffee, and fifteen

pounds of tea—genuine *Kaiser's-Thee.* What shall I do?" and he wrung his hands in terror.

" *Malchi,* hold your tongue," said the lady with an imperative tone, which showed she had not lived so long in Russia for nothing, " and listen."

The whole party now stood in silence, broken only by Rose, who in a low whisper related that she had seen that figure on the cliffs as they came in ; " but," she innocently added, " I took him for the *Sudār* (the Master) of the house himself."

The gravity of this declaration ruffled that of the lady for a moment ; but now all ears were again bent in the direction of the door, where apparently a parley not of the most amicable description was going forward ; while by the repeated jingle of the sledge-bells, the head of the little black horse in question seemed to be the object of contention.

Meanwhile the anxious thought, " Where can I hide these poor creatures?" was uppermost in the lady's mind.

In vain did she ransack the house from the *Boden,* as the provincial Germans improperly call their garret, to the cellar, for a safe asylum for them, when suddenly she exclaimed, " Stay ; I have thought of an excellent hiding-place ; here, good Tina, take my keys and lock these poor people up in the *Schafferei ;* that's the last place in which they'll fancy I should hide a hungry Jew."

Despite her terror, for all present partook of it, the good old soul received the keys with a somewhat humorous smile. But Axina, who had stood crossing herself most indefatigably, now changed the action into one of genuine secular wonderment at a proceeding on her mistress's part, no less foolhardy in her eyes than that of turning a ravenous wolf into a sheep-fold. Her indignation however was superfluous ; for before the order could be executed the *Strandreiter* shot like an arrow past the window, and his horse's hoofs were heard in diminishing thunder upon the hollow rocks.

" *Slāva Bōgu !*" " Thank God !" simultaneously ejaculated the Jewess and the English mistress, each in their native tongue.

And now all shyness vanished : the peasants thronged into the apartment, each ready to tell the tale where all seemed anxious alike to listen ; and though somewhat varying in detail, yet each agreeing in the main point, viz. that the danger was not over, but only suspended. The *Strandreiter*, it appeared, finding himself powerless against so many, had hurried off to the guard-house to bring up his comrades, and a strong band might be expected within an hour.

" The Russian dog wanted to drive the horse and sledge away," said one long-haired individual.

" If it had not been for our harpoons, more than one of us would have felt the point of his lance," said another.

" He tried to stab the horse in his fury," said a third.

" No, no," cried two or three voices at once ; " 'twas the sledge into which he stuck his pike."

" And no bad thought either," added the elder-looking of the party ; " how else should he know it again ?   But don't let us be talking and doing nothing ; that won't help the *Praua*,* and she is in the most trouble."

" Take my advice, *Praua*," said another, " and send the Jew, horse and sledge, bag and baggage, wife and child, into the woods. May be they 'll manage to keep clear of the Cossacks, though 'tis true Ivān's eyes are as sharp as his lance."

This prudent appeal remained unanswered ; for she to whom it was addressed seemed hardly to hear it.   But the Jew had understood all ; and with instinctive caution and trembling hands began securing and doing up the scattered contents of his pack, whose defenceless state in such a mixed company seemed not a little to aggravate his sufferings ; while Axina, seizing the opportunity, drove such a hard bargain for that same red and yellow cotton as no Jew in his senses would ever have consented to.

Meantime the lady still kept silence, engaged apparently in a painful conflict with herself, while the wild-looking peasants, who in their eagerness and vehemence had ventured nearer a superior than custom usually allowed, now sunk back, enframing her graceful figure in a semicircle which none seemed disposed again to cross.   But Rose was the first to break the ring : moving forward with a determined air, though paler than ever, one hand propping her child, she laid the other in its tattered sleeve upon the lady's arm : " Do not be in trouble for us ; we thank

* Mistress, a corruption of the German word *Frau*.

you for your kind words, and for the bread we have eaten under your roof: there are not many here who would have given us either. Come, husband, let us go into the woods; it is not so very cold; and the Lord Jehovah, who did not forsake the little Ishmael in the desert, will care for our Matvei. Come,"—and so saying she hugged the little bale of rags, which had sunk to sleep on her bosom, closer to her, and moved towards the door.

"No, no, Rose—stay," said the lady, grasping her by the collar of the wretched cloak; "I was not thinking of my own risk—no, indeed I was not. But—my husband—if he should return "—and here she stopped.

"I understand you, Sudārina; I would rather be in the cold woods with Matvei, than see you stand in fear before your lord. Let us go."

At these words the same elderly peasant—a plain but sensible-looking man, with awkward muscular person and long reddish locks, every hair of which curled separate with exposure to the frost—now stepped forward. "May your servant, Maddis, speak?"

"Speak, good Maddis," said his mistress; "you never speak idly."

"Then my advice is that you keep neither the Jew nor his wife here. I would say the same if they were Christians. It is not alone that the *Herr* will be angry, but the house will be ransacked; and where would you hide them then? It would not so much matter if we had another to deal with; for I would engage with a few roubles, or a couple of young lambs, or even half-a-dozen chickens, with *Praua's* permission, to make these Russians so blind that they should not know this Jew from old Jūrri the fire-lighter, or his pack there from a pile of billet-wood; but Ivān is not to be settled thus—honesty is his best line of cheating now. Is n't there a fresh order come to keep a stricter watch than ever? I 'll answer for it those Finlanders knew that well enough—but what won't a Jew risk for gain? (the Jew groaned)—And for the first smuggler he can catch, Ivān is to have a sum of money—to say nothing of an order to hang on his breast—which, to be sure, is more show than profit —as well as all the contraband he can lay his hands upon."

Here the Jew groaned again.

"If," said the lady eagerly, "it is nothing more than the goods, I'd willingly pay—"

"Oh! *Praua*, all your paying will do no good: the Russian would take the money first and the goods afterwards; and the poor creatures, though they were over-silly to put themselves in such a strait and the *Praua* in such trouble, would be sent on to St. Petersburgh; and many have walked to Siberia for a less crime than cheating the customs. And it is not unpunished either that they would get out of Ivān's grasp; for he is too fond of the fist and the whip among his own people to spare smugglers, whether man or woman—to say nothing of their being Jews, which makes the business ten times worse."

"What is to be done, then?" said the lady, shuddering at the thought. "I cannot bear to turn them out, especially this young creature," and she still kept her hold on Rose.

"Why, to be sure," said the old man, looking at the tender cheek of the Jewess with a pitying glance, "it seems hard to turn such a young wife into the woods, to eat birch-twigs and drink snow-water, but depend upon it, *Praua*, she is safer under God's roof than under man's. However, I have thought of a plan: we three here, Jūhann, Tomas," pointing to the two other peasants, "and myself, are ready for seal-hunting; let the Jew and his wife come with us; it will be hard if we can't land them at Hochland before six hours are over; it is not noonday yet. They are safe there; and when the Cossacks are tired of searching, can come back again at their leisure: or if they have to be out one night, it is only sleeping in their sheepskins as we do; besides, it is easy walking on the ice, and all downhill to it."

"But you will be seen from the cliff."

"What with this snow, *Praua*?" said the man, smiling; "no, nor even without it. We shall be as invisible before we have gone a quarter of a werst as a white hare on the plain."

"But what will become of my pack?" said the pedlar in an anxious tone, looking as if he would himself willingly have crept into it.

"I'll take care of that," said Maddis, to whom the contrivance was apparently no new experiment. "Here you, Mart, run with it, and you others help him, to that part of the wood where the ant-hills stand so thick; pile it up with a little snow, and no one will know it from its neighbours: the lady can have it fetched when the alarm is over."

"And I'll put the horse in the stable," said one voice.

"And I'll stow the sledge away where there are twenty like it," said another.

"But take the board out first where the lance pricked it, and into the fire with it," said Maddis again.

And now the lady, albeit not unused to those painful dilemmas where the heart and the judgment pull contrary ways, stood in deep consideration, whilst many an expectant look hung upon her determination. But though the main question seemed still irreconcileable in her mind, yet a little under-current of thoughtfulness had full play, and turning to the housekeeper, she gave directions in a low voice to fetch the bread and salt fish, which form the staple food of the lower orders, and a couple of bottles of brandy, and other provisions, adding, "they will want them wherever they go."

Her good sense told her that Maddis's plan in truth was the best and the most merciful; and for the pedlar, trained like every Russian to bear all weathers and stand all fatigues, she felt no compunction; but she wavered when she looked at the slight form and pale brow of the Jewess. The decision, however, was not to come from her.

"Rose," she began, "your husband will do well to accept this offer."

"The Sudārina is right."

"But you—you had best stay here, and it will be hard if I cannot protect you."

"No," said the young woman with a firm look. "The Sudārina means it well; but I go with my husband, were it to Siberia."

A short pause ensued.

"My heart bleeds for you, Rose, but I cannot dissuade you; you are right, and God be your help; but there is another duty for you yet."

The Jewess looked up imploringly, and with quickened breath, as if dreading, yet foreknowing the next word, and involuntarily pressed the sleeping child to her.

"Yes, *Bēdnaya* (poor one), you have guessed my meaning,—

you must leave your child here. I pity you from my very heart, but indeed you *must*; he would only encumber your steps, and you would surely not expose his tender life to the hardships you may perhaps undergo."

The Jewess's tears were falling fast upon the cheek of the slumberer. "Nay, put your trust in God,—the God of us all; with His blessing you will be back in a few days; and Matvei shall be as one of my own children. I won't be a bad mother to him," she said, trying to smile; "let me take him."

The Jewess did not articulate a word, or could not; but slowly and clumsily she was unfolding the bandages by which the child hung before her, and with every loosened knot seemed to be tearing her heart-strings asunder. At length the child lay free from all support, save only her circling arms, which were cold and blue with the absence of that blood which seemed to be choking her heart. She did not trust herself to kiss it, but with a solemnity which gave her young features an unnatural expression, she laid her treasure on the bosom of the English lady.

"May the Lord do unto your children as you do unto my Matvei, and may you never know"——here her voice failed, and turning away, she walked rapidly to the door.

But the transition from the damp rough folds that hung over the mother's breast, to the delicate linen which covered the fair round shoulder of the Englishwoman, had disturbed the slumberer, and opening his deep blue eyes to the strange face and folded tresses of the stranger, he set up a cry which the lady as quickly tried to stifle with the handkerchief with which she had wiped her own unconscious tears. Short and low as was that sound, the mother's ear had caught it; and now, as if beyond all power of self-control, back she bounded like an animal who hears the call of its young.

"Oh! Matvei! Matvei! *Moya Düschinka! moi Golübtschik!* how could I leave you!—I, your own mother, who never left you for a moment before!" And then suddenly seizing the lady, who had with difficulty hindered her from resuming the infant, with a convulsive grasp, "Oh! Sudárina! Sudárina! take him away, if you would not see my heart break,—take him away. I can't follow the father with Matvei before my eyes. I can't—I can't—"

nd here the good housekeeper interposing, led the poor distressed creature away; and the lady with her strange burthen escaped from this trying scene.

At the head of the stairs she was met by a little hazel-eyed couple of her own, who in their anxiety to see what little wailing *Pailo,* or baby, it was that their mother was carrying in her arms, were completely blind to the signs of agitation which her countenance still exhibited. Not so, however, the old Lena, their nurse, who, remarking that something had occurred to distress her mistress, received the little Matvei, and with him the injunction to give him food and put him on better clothing, without a question; adding only parenthetically, "and the *Pailo* will be none the worse for a little washing also."

"And take the children with you as well, Lena; I would rather be alone."

At this, the little rosy pair, who seldom found their mother so hard-hearted, evinced great symptoms of dissatisfaction; but while one was gradually pumping up a silent tear, and the other, with its little jaws at full stretch, was indulging in that ominous pause which invariably precedes a stout roar, Lena, assisted by Axina, who had followed her mistress, brushed and hushed them before her, and the door was relentlessly slammed upon their sorrows.

Indeed their mother required a little solitude, for she was wrought up to a pitch of anxiety for which the occasion seemed scarcely commensurate. Walking hurriedly up and down the long suite of apartments, she alternately stopped at one of the many windows facing the descent to the sea, or at one of those at the end of the house, which commanded the whole length of the cliff leading to the guard-house.

Long as this scene has taken to relate, it had occupied only a few minutes in occurrence; but each minute seemed doubled and trebled, and she was in a fever till the party should be gone. She listened,—her own heart's throb overpowered every other sound,—and then she heard the voices of the peasants below; but no one issued from the house. More than once she was tempted to return down stairs and expedite their flight. What could they be about? As often as she was disappointed on the one side, she turned restlessly to the other, and looked with straining eyes along the cliff, more than once fancying she could discern the figures of those horsemen who would effectually cut off their retreat. But no, this was impossible ; and the shapes that looked like the advancing *Strandreiters* were only the joint fruits of her own fears and the unsteady view which the slowly falling flakes afforded.

At length voices were heard without the house ; then the creaking noise of many footsteps on the frozen snow, and the party emerged at a brisk pace from beneath the windows. Three peasants, Maddis, Jūhann, and Tomas, loaded with their pikes and accompanied by a dog, took the lead ; the Jew and another figure followed, which latter, except for its smaller size, could hardly have been recognised for that of a woman. It was evident that the worthy Tina had cast her own sheepskin, which man and woman wear alike in this part of Russia, round the too thinly clad person of the Jewess, while the turban was covered with a heavy handkerchief, which effectually concealed its shape. The pedlar looked back and bowed to the window with his *fouraschka* to the ground, while Rose walked stoically on, as if she feared even to take a last look at the house where she had left her treasure.

And now they plunged into the wood, and the lady at her lofty window began to breathe more freely. If they had but time allowed them to gain the ice, they would, she felt, be safe from pursuit. The snow fell in flakes few and far between ; in a few minutes she saw them emerge from the thicket upon the second cliff, and descending again, were again hidden from view. Still her heart palpitated with fear, for the snow now cleared most inauspiciously away ; the landscape had all the hard distinctness which a freezing atmosphere imparts, and her belief in Maddis's prediction began to flag. She determined not to be impatient, but with ear and eye incessantly intent, now in the direction of the sea, now listening for the first hollow sounds on the cliff, patience and impatience seemed to assume much the same form. In a less time, however, than she had thought it possible, she distinctly saw their five figures, one behind the other, issue from the lowest wood, cross the line of flat beach, and now move so smoothly and unvaryingly in a north-western direction, as showed their footing was on the flat Baltic.

"Thank God ! so far," she exclaimed ; and then as quickly correcting herself, added in a low voice, "and come what may, thanks be to Him who ordereth all things on earth for the best."

Still her eyes watched those diminishing figures, whose progress upon the white, boundless, objectless desert, seemed as slow as that of the shadow on the dial. The island of Hochland lay clear upon the horizon; alas! how many weary steps were before them ere they should have passed along that imaginary line which her eye was perpetually tracing between them and its distant mountainous outline. Crusted with the frozen snow, they were already receding fast from her sight; and when she shut her eyes for a moment to ease them from the painful strain and glare, it was with difficulty she could recover the objects of her solicitude.

And now the children were re-admitted—all sorrow forgotten in the acquisition of a little companion: while Matvei, dressed in a last year's suit of the youngest child, tottered slowly between them, his cheeks so bright, and his eyes so beautiful, that old Lena—who, mistrusting somewhat his two officious little supporters, whose tender caresses, *en chemin*, had already more than once tripped him up, kept firm hold behind—declared no lady in the land need be ashamed to own him. This was the more flattering as coming from one who, like most old nurses, rarely praised any children but her mistress's. The lady took the child on her knee, and felt that he would soon claim her interest on his own as well as on his mother's behalf: and then, by a quick transition of thought, bending her eye on the icy expanse, she sought in vain for the vanished figures of his parents.

But short space, however, was allowed for self-gratulation; the noise of hoofs was now heard, and so near, that but for the children's prattle they must long have been audible. Rising to the window she perceived no less than eight horsemen advancing at a rapid pace. "Our brave peasants have inspired them with some respect, however," she murmured to herself. At about a hundred yards from the house they halted, and seemed to be taking a survey of the panorama around them. Involuntarily her looks again sought the Gulf, but, somewhat with a smile of derision at her own fears, she as quickly withdrew them; to all outward sense the fugitives existed not; while, as if to make security doubly sure, a thin veil of snow began to obscure the scene.

And now her native spirit arose: and gaining strength from the very reaction of her feelings, the Englishwoman secretly acknowledged to herself, that but for the dictates of prudence, she felt infinitely more disposed to defy the military party than to fear them. Perceiving that they had now encompassed the house, she summoned Tina, and gave orders that no impediment should be put in the way of their search, and no unnecessary word spoken to them.

"There are not many tongues left to speak," said the good soul, who greatly relished a dry joke, and was not far behind her lady in spirit; "all the men are off," she said, "except the *Wăhhamees* (the fire-lighter), and he is deaf; and Tonno the cook, and he speaks so seldom, he might be dumb; and the maids, God bless them! they are frightened out of their wits—not a head will be lifted from the spinning-wheels, I warrant."

"So much the better," said the mistress; "but if you want a tongue, here's a Russian one will speak for all. Nay, *Dyĕvuschka* (maiden), don't pout;" for Axina began to whimper and enumerate in rising tones the many indignities of the day; "if you have nothing worse to put up with through life but a few good-humoured jokes, you will be a favoured woman—I trust you may always earn your wages as honestly. Come to me for the keys, Tina, when you want them, and keep up your heart."

And here, having dismissed the children to their noontide slumber, she assembled her maidens around her, and applied herself to quiet occupation.

The Cossacks now seriously began their inquisitorial errand. Stationing a soldier at the back and front entrance of the house, so as to intercept all egress, they dismounted from their horses, and entered the extensive stables and outhouses. Here, however, nothing met their search but herds of quadrupeds—sheep and oxen—housed from the winter in commodious buildings, who continued to feed from their well-filled cribs, and looked at the intruders with perfect indifference.

In the stables they had no better success. The Jew's little nag was there, it is true, but safe from recognition among a multitude of a similar race; while the same might be said of the simple sledges, all so entirely in one fashion, that it seemed rather a mystery how the owners themselves should recognise them. Before half an hour had elapsed the party quitted this fruitless cover and approached the house; and in a few minutes the scraping of feet and jingling of spurs, mingled with authoritative tones, were heard below. Soon the housekeeper re-appeared: " The keys, *Praua*—quick—the keys of the cellar and the *Schafferei;* I should not wonder if they broke the locks whilst I am away."

" Here they are, good Tina; keep close at their heels, and don't lock them in, as I proposed doing with the poor Jews, or my spirit-bottles will soon be emptied." Tina showed her white teeth from ear to ear, and bustled away.

After much banging of doors, and several very audible oaths in good Russian, the noise approached the staircase: in a few seconds the doors of the apartment were flung wide open, and half a dozen wild-looking, moustachioed fellows, with long pikes and long cloaks, rushed in, preceded by one who, from his fero-cious looks, it required no stretch of imagination to recognise as the much-dreaded Ivān. From the swaggering confidence with which this individual entered, it seemed as if he entertained little doubt of daunting every being in his progress: what was his surprise, then, on finding himself in a private room, the doors shut on all sides, and in the presence of a quiet woman, who, occupied with her servants at a respectful distance round her, took no notice whatever of his entrance! As much from em-barrassment as from a species of respect, the Cossack now took off his cap; and the lady, fixing her keen eye upon him, mildly inquired what he wanted. But the awe which, in common with every Russian, he evinced in presence of a superior was but momentary, and with some insolence he replied, that he was come to search the house for some concealed criminals, and search it he would, were a regiment to oppose him. Without vouch-safing him an answer she turned to two of the servants, desiring them to show the Cossacks round every apartment, and to let them search where they pleased. " But before I allow a door to be opened," she said, addressing herself to the soldiers, " I de-mand that you lay down your pikes; there are none here to oppose you, unless Russian soldiers are afraid of women and children: the former I desire you will not annoy, and the latter I should advise you, for your own sakes, not to awaken."

At these last words a titter ran through the household group, and even the hard features of the soldiers looked as if they would have gladly relaxed. With instinctive obedience they now began to lay down their pikes, while their leader, met by different weapons than he had ever been accustomed to oppose, looked as if he knew not quite what next to do, and offered no opposition to the act. Then, as if desirous to drown all sense of this rather humiliating interlude by the noisiest resumption of authority, he suddenly sent them off to the right and left with a few hearty imprecations, himself remaining where he could overlook their proceedings, and at the same time keep guard over the lady, whom he watched as closely as if he suspected the criminals to be lying *perdus* in some fold of her graceful *capote*.

Meanwhile his followers set about their business in the true spirit of Russian custom-house minions ; and if their zeal may be measured by the closeness of their search, it was certainly of the most loyal description. Not content with searching every possible, and many somewhat impossible places of concealment, they proceeded to open boxes, ransack drawers, and peep into holes and corners, where a man, if, like the ostrich, so inclined, might perhaps have contrived to hide his head, but certainly could have introduced no other portion of his person. Nevertheless, it is but fair to record that these works of supererogation seemed dictated rather by stupidity than by malice : they were satisfied with spoiling, only in one sense of the word ; and whether deterred by fear, or sore hindered by the sharp eyes of the attendant housemaids, the party abstained from all actual pilfering. Their steps now led to the nursery door, which also opened at their bidding, and before they quitted this sanctuary that sequel ensued which the lady had hinted at ; and all the little voices were in a chorus, in which Matvei, whose lineage they little suspected, took no inconsiderable part.

In about half an hour the soldiers rejoined their chief with tidings of their lack of success. Foiled in every respect, Iván again levelled a few of those denunciations at his men, which, in the Russian service, are as frequent in the mouths of the officers as the words of command ; and then himself strided through the apartments, gratuitously pulling down, it is said, a few curtains and smashing a partition, and even converting old Lena into his everlasting foe by wantonly maltreating an old rickety nursery-chair by which she set great store. Finding nothing could be done, he now returned to his post, and in a manner which evidently anticipated no refusal, demanded, more than requested, that provisions and brandy should be served to himself and his men. But Iván had greatly mistaken the character of the lady. " Provisions for you and your men !" she exclaimed, her eyes flashing fire, and the angry blood rising to her cheek ; " not a morsel of bread nor drop of water shall ye receive at my hands. When I bid such visitors to my board they shall not complain of lack of hospitality, but unbidden guests must bring their own entertainment. Think not to extort anything from the servants ; I have the keys of all here," pointing to a weighty bunch which lay beside her, " and touch them or me at your peril. No, go your ways, the sooner the better ; and beware how you again take advantage of the absence of the master to trouble a peaceful house. There are those at my bidding who will not leave it unpunished."

At these very unequivocal words, the barbarian, who, partly from his station, but chiefly from the name his brutality had acquired, was accustomed to see all flee before him with fear or meet him with propitiation, stood a few seconds paralyzed with astonishment, uncertain, apparently, whether to pocket the affront or to spike the lady. But knowing in his own heart that there were those who could as easily work his destruction as he that of those beneath him, and uneasy beneath that eye which now followed his every movement, he marshalled his troop together, venting indistinct imprecations and threats on them, on the fugitives, and on all around him ; and finally eased the immediate pressure of his rage by sending one unfortunate member of his corps at a quicker pace down the stairs than the regulations of marching strictly required.

Quickly after the trampling of horses' feet was heard, and the troop rode off different ways, leaving a couple of their party patrolling before the house.

Quiet now speedily returned to the mansion. The lady immediately repaired to her nursery, while her train of maidens proceeded to restore order in those apartments where the scrutiny had been the severest. Many and loud were the lamentations, especially from Axina, whose department had been most particularly invaded ; and in the fulness of her heart she made her way to her mistress's side laden with various articles, or bits of

M

articles, which had been broken or dirtied beneath the clumsy fingers of the Cossacks, and was disappointed, rather than the contrary, to find the lady's cheerfulness proof to all this catalogue of misfortunes. Sitting with Matvei on her lap, and her own little ones pressing around her knees, she only replied, "Never mind, Axina, a few hours will put all to rights; we may be thankful to have escaped so well ; they can have but few real griefs who can afford to be unhappy about trifles. No, my little fellow ! if your poor parents be but safe, we won't repine, will we ?" said the lady, accompanying her words with those particular looks and sounds which are supposed to be most intelligible and agreeable to little babies. To which kind appeal little Matvei only drooped the corners of his mouth, looked her piteously in the face, and ejaculated in his most plaintive tones, " *Gde Maminka ?*" " Where 's mamma ?"

After the unusual excitement of the morning, the afternoon passed slowly away. Often did the lady's thoughts follow the fugitives and their trusty guides, and often did she open the small double pane which alone admits air into a Russian apartment, and put out her delicate hand or graceful head to ascertain the temperature. The snow had ceased, and the evening stole on light and milder than usual, the most propitious seemingly to her wishes. Nevertheless an undefined feeling of anxiety hung over her, which she felt was ungrateful, but could not dispel ; and knowing that activity of the body is more hopeful on such occasions than all the reasoning of the mind, she set about various household affairs, superintended her children's evening meal, and then applied herself to consider how she should best do her duty by the little stranger committed to her care without infringing upon any other. For she was not one of those who in the hurry to perform the latest new duty neglect fifty prior ones, and thus only indulge one of the many forms of selfishness. To her husband the presence of one child more or less in the lower story would, she knew, be perfectly indifferent, if not unknown ; for in great houses of this description it is thought quite natural that the married servants should live in the bosom of their families as well as their lords, who frequently indeed take no census at all of their household population. But the case became widely different if the attempt were made to introduce a child of low degree, and that, moreover, a Jew, among the ranks of the little aristocrats above. Nor was she to be misled by any pleadings of mistaken kindness. It was soon decided therefore in her mind that the little boy should be made over to the care of her trusty housekeeper, and to the companionship of her rising generation, for Tina had as many olive-branches as her mistress. This transfer became also the more imperative, as the poor little fellow, whom the wonder and the novelty had at first chiefly kept mute, now began to wail and call for his distant mother in tones which were most distressing to the elder, and somewhat contagious to the younger, inmates of the upper story.

At the lady's behest, therefore, the good woman appeared; but she looked so woe-begone, and sighed so deeply as she perceived the little Matvei sitting on her mistress's lap, that the lady, more out of fear of being tempted to give way to kindred feelings herself than from any displeasure, could not refrain from a kind reprimand.

"What's this, Tina? I don't know what ails you all. Here is Axina can't forgive me for not making myself unhappy, now that the danger is over, and you seem just as unreasonable. Come, cheer up, and be thankful that the poor people got safe away at all; by this time they must be nearing their journey's end."

"God grant it!" murmured the housekeeper in a solemn tone, her very cap trembling with emotion; while her mistress, unheeding these signs, proceeded to give her various injunctions about Matvei's installation and accommodation down stairs, winding up with a few precepts regarding supper, which, though they had been duly recited before, most mistresses think the better for repetition. "Well, good night, Tina,—take the poor child,—I think he will be quieter with you than with me; but stay, let me kiss his soft cheek. Why, Tina! you are *crying*!" And in truth, as if the touch of the child had opened some fount of sympathy, the good creature now sobbed as if her heart would break.

"Nay, you are upset with what we have gone through to-day; here, take a cup of tea (this being a beverage a Russian servant rarely tastes), it will do you good." But, refusing the boon more by gesture than words, the faithful woman broke away, and little Matvei's wail was heard below.

The next morning, after a night of troubled dreams, all bearing upon the late occurrence, the lady awoke from a slumber, which, without recurring to clock or watch, she instantly felt had been extended much beyond the usual hour. As she started up, her eye fell on the figure of the housekeeper standing by her bed. " You here, Tina ! Where 's Axina ? How could she let me sleep so long ?"

" *Ya sdez*, I here," said that damsel in a most plaintive voice. By this time the fair delicate feet had emerged from their warm covering, and one already rested on the floor, when, struck by the silence of her attendants, she suddenly looked up, and found them both gazing at her with a peculiarly mournful expression. In an instant the conviction rushed to her mind that some misfortune had occurred which they were concealing from her. " What 's the matter ?   What has happened ?   I know something has happened," she said, in an agitated tone.   " Are the children all well ?   Has the *Herr* met with an accident ?   Speak, Axina ! Tina ! speak this moment !"   There was nothing in the looks or tones of either to comfort her, but the Tina hastened to assure her of the perfect health of her children,— who, indeed, were pretty audible,—and the equal safety of the Herr, as far as she, his servant, knew.

" But 'tis for the poor child that the Praua will be troubled— His poor parents !......" here she paused.

" Go on ! go on ! What of them ? They are not taken ?   How could I think of my own first !"

" That was but natural," observed the good woman, " and right, too."   And then, with tears starting from eyes that appeared not to have closed all night, she added, " No, they are not taken ; would to heaven they were ; no matter what came of it.   But no,—I can't tell the Praua,—I can't, indeed.   Juhann will be here soon."

" Juhann ! What of him ? Is he back ? Tell me. Speak, one of you !"

" Oh, Praua ! 'tis a sad tale ;—the ice ! Praua ; and the poor creatures have not above one day's provisions. . ."

"The ice ! What do you mean ? How you torment me ! Speak !"

" Oh, Praua ! 'tis because I am loath to grieve you ;—but *the ice is broken up, and the Gulf is open !*"

Without answering a word, barefooted as she was, the lady flew through the adjoining room, Axina in vain endeavouring to overtake and throw a shawl round her thinly clad person, till she reached one of the windows commanding the sea. The double glass obscured her sight. Regardless of the cold, she flung open the double pane, and distinctly perceived, beyond the miles of ice which encompassed the shore, a space of open and gloomy waters, in which the island of Hochland floated as free from ice as in summer. The appalling truth now flashed upon her. By one of those rare movements, when winds and hidden currents combine, not known once in twenty years, the sea had indeed cleared itself of its main ice in the space of one night; and the poor fugitives! where were they? . . .

"Poor Juhann could get no further than the forester's cottage last night, and the forester himself came up and told me the disaster before I came upstairs to Praua."

"Last night! Oh, why did you not tell me? Something might have been done."

"All was done, Praua, that the hand of man could do. I thought the sad news would come soon enough upon you this morning;" for Tina had lived with her young mistress from her arrival in this country, and cherished her like a child of her own. "Sleep is a blessed thing; and the heart wants it as much as the body. I had rest of neither last night, I am sure; and the poor child wailing all the while for his mother."

And here the retrospect of her own woes loosened poor Tina's last powers of self-control, and, sobbing out that she would bring Juhann upstairs the moment he came, she left the room.

"I'll be ready," said the lady. "Quick, Axina, and dress me." But Axina did not understand being hurried; her heart and her fingers were quite separate concerns; and though doubtless the one sympathized deeply for her mistress's distress, the others stirred not a bit the quicker for all her impatience. At first this was borne with tolerable composure, but when, at her customary leisurely pace, she proceeded to gather up the long shining tresses which hung almost to the floor, the lady's patience was fairly exhausted. Snatching them out of her grasp, she coiled them round with her own trembling hands, and unheeding all Axina's remonstrances on their being "*sovsem krivoi*,"—

"all awry," she completed her toilette just as Tina reappeared with Juhann himself.

The poor man was apparently suffering as much in body as in mind; his face and limbs were swollen with exposure to the cold, and it was with difficulty that he gave the following account.

It appeared that the party had proceeded on their way at a good speed, and with cheerful spirits; the track being uninterrupted, save by a few cracks of no importance, and by occasional holes of deep water, which at all times occur; and where the party had loitered to secure two seals, which they left lying where they had killed them. The light drifting snow which blew from the land obscured the view before them; nevertheless they apprehended no impediment, and it was to the surprise of the most experienced, and to the consternation of the whole party, that they found themselves, after what seemed to them a walk of about eighteen wersts, stopped by open sea. They now resolved to return at all hazards, and, for the Jew's sake, land higher up; but the wind from the land side increased and greatly fatigued them, and they had not retraced their steps above half an hour, when they were further appalled by that dull crashing sound which accompanies the separation of large fields of ice, and redoubling their speed, found themselves again arrested by open water. On all sides now the ice began to shift, and after desperate but fruitless attempts to escape in a northern or southern direction, it became apparent that they were enclosed upon a floating mass, not less than from three to four wersts in circumference, and separated by about half a werst from the main ice which encompassed the shore. By the advice of Maddis, Juhann, being an experienced diver and swimmer,—the only one of the party indeed who could swim at all,—now determined to commit his warm life's blood to the benumbing waters, as much to secure the nearest chance for his own escape, as to provide means, by alarming others, for saving the rest of the party. Casting off, therefore, his heavy sheepskin and all the garments he could spare, and leaving his harpoon and bag of bread, he encouraged his companions with the hopes of succour, and flung himself in. More than once he feared he must sink in the icy fluid, so paralysing was the effect upon his limbs; and when, after incredible efforts, he dashed himself on a promontory of ice which stretched in a narrow line towards him, and looked back upon the group, he became aware that the distance between them and the shore had greatly increased. Benumbed and exhausted, he now made his way along with great difficulty,—often obstructed by deep rents which obliged him to make a circuit,—and at length succeeded in reaching the forester's cottage. All the peasants in the vicinity were now collected, and bearing a *jolle*, or light boat, they repaired immediately to the ice in the direction he indicated, but found its surface shifting and subdividing so quickly, and altogether so insecure to traverse, that it was with difficulty they could themselves return.

" God help the poor creatures!" added Juhann, after he had finished his oft-interrupted recital ; " but it is hard a Christian should share the curse upon a Jew. The Praua had better have given them up !"

The lady was silent, for she knew this was no time to strive with prejudices ; and indeed her heart was so surcharged with feelings of grief and commiseration that she hardly heard the concluding speech. The same might be said of a conversation which ensued between Tina and Juhann, where, in the true spirit of homely consolation, they mutually told anecdotes of fishermen and seal-hunters who had been carried out to sea on detached masses of ice, and never heard of again ; whereby, if prejudice were ever consistent, it might have struck Juhann that it pleases the Almighty to send the curse of such inflictions no less upon the Christian than upon the Jew.

At this moment, as if to fill the cup of misery to the brim, the wail of little Matvei, with his wretched " *Gde maminka ! gde maminka !*" was heard in the next room ; when, as if responsible to the child for the inactivity in which she had hitherto stood, the lady hurriedly and incoherently proposed and urged various schemes for recovering the unfortunate party, all hopeless or impracticable, and serving little more than to show the agitation of the mind whence they proceeded ; and then, rushing into the next room, she snatched up the orphan child in her arms, and wept over him as bitterly and passionately as if she had been his own mother, and the little warm frightened being on her bosom a cold inanimate corpse. To those of her household nearest her person, who had been accustomed to guess at their mistress's sorrows rather by what she concealed than by what she exhibited, the aspect of her present passionate grief seemed a new feature in her character. But they knew not what she, poor lady! could best have told ; namely, that the very school of sorrow, in which, after Divine aid, the sense of self-sacrifice is the only support, and the practice of strict duty the only relief, leaves the heart more than usually susceptible and defenceless to the blows which fall on another. But soon the habit of self-control returned, and the very hopelessness of human aid, the very sense of incapacity to help them, under which her benevolent spirit at first gave way, led her more closely to that Power, without whom no human aid, however near and prompt, could have been availing. Anxious now only to discharge every obligation which this misfortune entailed, she sought the families of her own two lost peasants, gave them help and sympathy, and found comfort in the reflection that only he who had been saved had the additional responsibility of husband and father. This done, her life resumed its accustomed quiet tenor. It cannot be said that the possibility of the ultimate rescue of Matvei's parents was utterly banished from her feelings ; but she subdued it with somewhat of the sternness of a mind trained, in self-defence, not to shrink from the fullest recognition of sorrow,—accustomed, in the words of the great poet, to

> " Espouse its doom, and cleave
> To fortitude, without reprieve."

*   *   *   *   *

And now we must quit this domestic scene and follow the fate of the fugitives. It was some hours before they gave up the hope of immediate escape from their forlorn situation, independent even of the promised assistance from the shore, for the currents drove them sometimes nearer to the beds of ice which bordered the strand ; but as evening drew on, the breeze from the shore freshened again, and the huge bark of ice drifted rapidly out to sea. Hitherto the dog, which belonged to Juhann, and which he had motioned back, had been the only complainer ; for seeing his master's receding figure, and comprehending perhaps by instinct the danger of their situation, he began to howl and whine most piteously, keeping guard at the same time upon the sheepskin which Juhaun had thrown off. Rose was the only one who attempted to comfort the poor animal ; patting and caressing him, she sat herself down close to the edge, looking steadfastly towards the diminishing square mass of the house upon the cliff, which remained distinct against the sky, as long as the sky itself had any light. But few words were exchanged ; the peasants, naturally taciturn in disposition, stood leaning on their pikes towards the centre of the floating field, occasionally sustaining a low dialogue, while the pedlar wandered restlessly between them and his wife, without addressing himself to either. The expression on the countenance of the Hebrew pair was widely different : the knit brow, the fever gathered on the cheek of the Jew, showed the anxiety that was preying within ; while Rose was pale, gentle, and quiet, like one accustomed to take and bear whatever necessity imposed upon her, equally without inquiring or even understanding its object. Seeing her husband near, she said, " Shall we soon reach the shore?" The Jew averted his face and answered something, but so indistinctly that she heard it not, and then walked towards the peasants. Shortly after the party called to her, and bade her come nearer the centre : " It is best to be in the middle of such an awkward raft, young wife," said Maddis ; " the edges will break away." Rose took up the sheepskin, to which the dog made no opposition, and followed by the animal joined the others.

They now produced their stores of provisions, each respectively eating his own, and then spreading the surplus sheepskin, arranged themselves in a sitting posture, back to back, and so determined to await the dawn. The night was mild, and, fatigued with their exertions, some of the party sunk to sleep. With the first streaks of morning Maddis arose, and, approaching the edge, stood with folded arms, his long locks waving in the wind. In a moment a step was at his side—it was the Jewess.

" When do you think we shall touch land again?" said she with a suppressed voice.

" Look around you, young wife," and as he said this he pointed not ungracefully to an horizon of waves which encompassed them ; " this is not a question for a poor man like me to answer : but *Jummala* * can do much !"

* God.

The Jewess groaned.

"This is rough work for a young thing like you. I thought you had been asleep."

"'T is but poor sleep the body can take when the heart is not at rest," answered Rose.

"You have left a *pailo* on shore," he added with abrupt sympathy. "Well, poor thing! your heart may well ache; a child is dearer than all, they say, though it was not God's will that I should have one.   But my old father and mother will look often across the Gulf and wish me back!"

"I pity your mother," said Rose, and then rejoined her husband; and instinctively clinging together, though without uttering a word of what they mutually felt, the unfortunate pair wandered desolately up and down.

The prospect before them was indeed gloomy.   Fixed upon a floating island which they had no means of directing,—sole tenants of the open sea,—all that remained to them was the vague hope of nearing one of the shores of the Gulf; for any chance of being picked up by a vessel at this season was utterly vain.   They drifted rapidly, apparently southward, and Maddis knew, though he said it not, that the further they were blown in that direction the less was their chance of escape.   The hours passed slowly away, and no sound broke the silence but the chafing of the waters against the icy walls.   The Jew seemed equally benumbed both in mind and body.   Shivering with cold he cast himself down upon the sheepskin, which all had now vacated, and there lay to all appearance asleep; while his wife, seated at his side, watched with vacant eye the movements of the two peasants, who from time to time endeavoured to pierce a seal which played round their float.   A second evening closed slowly around them;—a second night wore wretchedly away;—still they drifted on.   Now came that trying period,—that racking, nervous impatience, when hope is forsaking the mind and apathy has not yet entered it,—when the heart has full scope to torture itself, before personal want stifles all reminiscence, and much of anticipation, in the sufferings of the creature.   What shipwrecked wretch, adrift on the wide ocean, has not known this crisis!—the last and worst agony of the mind before that of the body begins, —and all the time nothing to do!   It is needless to say that this, like other awful occasions, is the test of individual character.

The Jew still kept his sullen position. Maddis watched round their prison to see that no other floating ice-mass should shiver it: his countenance expressed much anxiety, but he spoke seldom, though always with kindness. Tomas, whose mind seemed of a low order, slept much, or sat with his head on his knees, listlessly picking holes with his harpoon in the ice, and teazing the dog by throwing the fragments at him. But Rose—poor creature!—she it was who suffered most at this stage. At times she sat motionless, her looks fixed on vacancy, one arm flung across her husband's breast, and sometimes her face hidden upon the same; then she would suddenly rise, as if a quiescent position were no longer endurable, and retreating to the edge, pace up and down with the restlessness and irritation of an animal before the bars of its cage. On one occasion her step was so hurried, her brow so flushed, and her actions so wild, that Maddis, fearing she would cast herself into the waters, seized her by the arm and endeavoured to draw her back to her husband. But she broke violently from him. " Don't hinder me,—don't hinder me," she said; " I know what I am about; I am not beside myself,—I wish I was,—may God forgive me! But when these fits of yearning come over me I cannot remain there; the aching heart is best carried on the restless foot."

" I'll rouse your husband; 't is a shame he does not try to comfort you."

" Try to comfort me!" said Rose with a bitter smile; " poor man! he has not the heart to look my misery in the face; and he suffers as much as I do; but the ways of sorrow are different with different men. No, no, Christian! there's no comfort for me: I must bear my portion alone," and she groaned aloud.

" There's comfort to be had," said Maddis solemnly, " but it depends upon the asking. *He* said this in whose mouth no guile was ever found; but I fear, poor afflicted creature! you know but little of Him."

" The Lord of Hosts is my refuge," said Rose meekly. " His strength it is which at times upholds me, but at others I hardly know what I say or do. My prayers are on my lips, but my Matvei is before my eyes,—my ears hear only his voice,—my arms stretch to meet him!——But no! I shall never, never again press him to this bosom!" and overcome with the violence of her grief, she folded her arms wildly as if to convince herself of the emptiness of her grasp, and then sinking on her knees, tears for the first time came to her relief.

After this she became more composed; her fits of tears were frequent, but her impatience was gone; and, with all a woman's consoling gentleness, this untutored being, subduing her own grief, applied herself to assuage the distress of her companions. Soon her husband required all her comfort and command of herself: rising from his recumbent posture, he wandered up and down with unsteady gait, as if stupified by a sorrow which found no natural vent. When their slender meal came round, he turned loathing from it, and refused to touch a morsel. In vain did poor Rose follow and beseech him to eat; he seemed, as she truly said, to turn his face from her.

" The hand of the Lord is heavy upon me! The hand of the Lord is heavy upon me!" he repeated. "Would that I had perished beneath the stripes of my enemies!"

" Nay, my husband," said the gentle woman, " let us not repine. Remember that it is better to fall into the hands of the living God than into the hands of man. Did not the pious king David, when he had sinned in the sight of the Lord, choose rather to see holy Israel fall by a wasting pestilence than by the swords of their enemies? Let us think of this and be comforted. Nay, cast me not off,—throw not your poor Rose from you; if she may not comfort her husband in the hour of affliction, it were better she were dead, for her other treasure is gone,"—and weeping she led him to the centre, and there gently compelled rather than persuaded him to sit down. In truth, he required all her tenderness, and her words respecting the choice of David were more literally true in their application than she had deemed; for wasting sickness was upon him, and may-be would have broken out wherever he might have been, though now accelerated by the agony of mind and exposure he had undergone. Burning fever now came on, and in a few hours this member of the miserable group was insensible to the peculiar wretchedness of his situation.

They had now been at sea five days, and as the cold and hungry

creatures looked at their slender stock of provisions, now so reduced as not to have served a hearty child for one meal, they
seemed to see the hours of their life numbered before them.
Urged by desperation, the looks of the younger man, whose disposition appeared only hardened by suffering, fell upon the dog.
Murmuring between his teeth that there was no use in keeping
the animal alive, that they could give him no food, and that if
they waited much longer he would give them none,—for the poor
dumb creature, though he had hitherto shared in Rose's portion,
was indeed reduced to skin and bone,—he approached with his
pike, at the same time holding out his hand and encouraging
it by name. But the intelligent animal seemed to know what
had been uttered, and, retreating before him, crouched at Rose's
side.

" *Tulli seya, Netta*—come here, Netta," he repeated, and
even held out a morsel of bread ; but no,—Netta was not to be
caught even by this tempting lure, and, irritated by opposition,
Tomas was advancing to seize the dog, when Rose stopped his
arm.

" Let the poor beast take its chance of life," said she ; " perhaps the Lord may hearken to our distress and give us food.
But don't kill him : let us all live or die together ; and the animal has not, like us, a life beyond."

" What does a Jew know of another life ?" said Tomas bru-
tally ; and still endeavouring to strike the dog, and still withheld
by Rose, he broke out into abusive epithets against her race.
But Rose was not to be daunted, and identifying the cause of the
poor dog with her own, she replied with more fire than any
would have attributed to her—

" And what do you know of the Hebrews ? There are as
many Hebrews as little like what you call Jews, as there are
Christians who act not up to the creed they profess ; and if you
Christians think your religion the better of the two, more 's the
shame. I have ever found those the best Christians who were
kindest to the Israelite. No—touch him not ; you shall strike
me sooner."

And it seemed by his actions as if the hard-hearted man would
not have hesitated to do this, when Maddis interfered.

" For shame, Tomas ! Let her alone, and the dog also. The

woman is right; no Christian could have spoken better. If she is not like us in knowing the Gospel truths, at all events we are all alike in needing them. I wish all Christians were as patient in times of affliction as she."

Rose's liquid eye was lifted up with an expression of gratitude to the rough, unshaven, and want-stricken features of Maddis, while Netta in his turn pressed close against her and gently licked her hands.

It seemed as if a blessing rested upon Rose's words; for ere another hour had elapsed Maddis succeeded in capturing a seal, and all angry feelings were banished at the sight of food. But even to his favourite sport Netta would not venture out, but laid close to Rose with pricked ears and wagging tail as he watched the booty.

They had drifted thus long in one direction, and according to their rough calculations were about abreast of the town of Pernau, when suddenly the wind changed, the cold sharpened, and heavy snow began to fall. By the violence of the waves their floating island now suffered; first the edges broke up and altered in shape, and then larger masses followed; till the poor castaways foresaw that this, their last stay, would vanish beneath them. The unconscious Jew was now dragged by the weakened hands of his companions into a more central part, and, before many hours, only a fragment of about four *Faden*, or twenty-four feet across, was left to them. As a last resource, Maddis and Tomas applied themselves to treading down the snow round the edges, by which they ensured a greater power of resistance. The love of life now kept one or other perpetually pacing round their diminished barrier, while the exercise revived their chilled circulation and even afforded slight relief to their minds. The seventh night now came on, and doubly wretched it was; for the wind blew hard, and the intense cold seemed as if it would perish their ill-fed bodies. The poor pedlar was the only creature who cared not for the change: in strange opposition with his companions he lay parched with fever, while Rose, melting the snow in her hands, dropped the water upon his lips from her emaciated fingers. Sometimes he scarcely appeared to breathe at all, and the poor wife may be forgiven for envying him his insensibility.

As the eighth morning dawned it became evident to their eager eyes that the horizon was broken by a line of elevated shore. This auspicious sight was hailed with a burst of wild joy by the three forlorn creatures, to whom the mere change of thought was a relief beyond what other happier mortals can conceive. And yet madly to dare to hope, when so many weary miles lay between them and the longed-for haven—when their only chance depended on the caprice of those very winds and currents of which they had hitherto been the sport, and when that escape, even were it within their reach, they, in their weakened state, had hardly the strength left to grasp—to hope thus merely because it was sweet to hope; thus wantonly to overthrow for a few hours of fallacious pleasure that habit of misery which had dulled its acuteness, that resignation which had been wrestled for with tears and anguish—this indeed seemed greater cruelty than all which had gone before. On the other hand, to repress that merciful feeling without which the life of man were worse than death—to deny the cravings of their own pining hearts—to steel their senses when a reprieve was in sight—this seemed crueler far, and was impossible.

The sun rose bright—the frost was intense—and the lights and shadows into which the rocky coast was thrown became gradually more distinguishable. As noon wore round, the sea sank—they floated slower and slower—and at length seemed to become stationary; and as evening approached, they owned to each other, less by words than looks of despair, that the wind had veered round, and that that distant shore, that harbinger of hope and peace to their failing hearts, that promise of food, warmth and rest to their famished bodies, was fast sinking below the horizon !

Who may now tell the agony of their feelings ! They seemed not to know how delicious had been that brief glimpse of hope, nor how far they had indulged it, till it was snatched from their grasp. Accents of despair, loud and bitter, now escaped from their lips, and even the pious Maddis flung himself prostrate upon the ice in miserable despondence.

*　　　*　　　*　　　*

The spring was unusually delayed in this latitude, or rather that nameless season which, in Russia, unites all the cold and immobility of winter with the sunny light and brightness of summer, was unusually protracted. It was not till the commencement of May that the currents in Nature's veins began again to circulate, that the rivers burst their bonds, and that the thundering sound of the ice as it loosened its hold from the shore was replaced by the gentle murmur of the waves. Meanwhile the inmates of the house upon the cliff were well and prosperous. The little interloper had advanced in the useful arts of talking and walking, thrived in health, grew in favour with all around him, and had apparently long forgotten his former condition. Gifted with great beauty, and endowed with a more than common share of childhood's witchery, he had found but little difficulty in establishing a footing on the upper story, and there became alternately the plaything and playfellow of his elder companions. Often as the lady stopped to look at the healthy gambols of the little party, her smile of maternal pleasure was checked by a sigh of regret, as she looked at Matvei and thought of the young and hapless mother who had borne and cherished him.

It was now warm summer weather; the earth had absorbed all the long-frozen stores of moisture, and the children's in-door sports were exchanged for a freer range; till one sultry day, returning heated and fatigued from more than usual activity in the garden, the little party crept languidly and willingly to their noonday couches, and Matvei, already deep asleep, was flung upon the lady's own bed. With their merry voices thus hushed, and hot noonday stillness reigning without, the lady retreated to her high west window, the scene from which was now clothed in all the tender colours of fresh verdure and hazy heat, relieved by the cool blue of the broad distant Gulf above. Her husband was again absent, or rather we must confess that it better suits our purpose to abstract him from the scene, to which (except of course in the eyes of his wife) he added no particular interest. She therefore sat alone, and her thoughts had wandered back to her own "loved isle in the west," when her eye was caught by two figures slowly rising above the most distant line of cliff, now disappearing, now emerging, as they wound through the thicket. It was a peasant in his long national coat, with a female figure at his side. As they came nearer, and as the ascent increased, they stopped from time to time, and the peasant helped the woman along with a kindness not often evinced by this class towards the weaker sex. There was something in the general appearance of the man which excited recollections in the mind of the lady. She arose and stooped forward out of the window, as if nearer to approach the object of her gaze. Surely! was it possible? could that be the living figure of Maddis Ploom? They came nearer—a dog preceded them; her heart beat with indefinable agitation. They were now close to the house. "Oh heavens! it can be no other!"—and clasping her hands to her forehead, as if mistrusting the evidence of her senses, the lady flew with the speed of mingled fear and hope down the stairs. The moment she entered the housekeeper's room her eye fell on the figure of Rose, whom Tina was endeavouring to support, and who now struggled with wild gestures to approach her. "Sudārina! Sudārina! my child—my Matvei!—take me to him. You don't speak," said the agitated young creature, and then perceiving the lady's cheeks were streaming with tears, and falling, as the human mind does, when in excessive tension, from the extreme of hope to equal despair, she screamed out, "He is dead! my child is dead! Oh! why was I spared?" and fell at her feet.

"Matvei is living," said a sweet voice above her, broken by sobs. "Matvei is alive and well! Come with me; lean on me, poor trembling creature!" But Rose raised herself up with convulsive strength, and with short and gasping breath hastened up the stairs and through the apartments which divided her from her treasure. As the lady opened the door of the sleeping-room she trembled so excessively that those behind were obliged to sustain her, and seemed almost incapable of meeting that moment which fulfilled her fondest desire. The room was darkened, but the lady flung back a curtain, and before them, flushed with sleep, its little lovely arms flung out in impatience of the heat, lay the blooming child. A pause ensued, in which Rose hung speechless over the unconscious cherub, and her thirsty heart seemed to drink a draught of long-yearned-for love. Still she stood—spell-bound—as if she feared by sound or touch to dispel the exquisite illusion before her. But the lady took one little plump hand in her's—the other was quickly raised to the opening

N

lids, and after a stare—half sleepiness, half wonder—from those full blue orbs, the child stretched out its arms to the Jewess, and cried " *Maminka!*"

We pass over the feelings of this moment: the Jewess's gratitude to the lady, which, with her artless admiration of the child's improved plight and beauty, burst from her lips between the intervals of her pressing him to her bosom; and the revulsion of sorrow, as in broken accents she related that Matvei had now no parent but herself. Her story was briefly this. After the ninth morning had dawned, when their last morsel was consumed, and they had given themselves over to utter hopeless misery, and thought themselves alike forsaken of God and man, they found themselves nearing the coast of Finland, were seen from the little island of Pilling, about twenty-five wersts from the mainland, and rescued after incredible exertions. But, as Rose touchingly said, " The Lord thought fit to establish in our hearts a remembrance of this affliction, that in the day of safety we might not again forget him. My poor husband recovered only to know he was safe, and died the second day after his landing."

As soon as the season permitted, and opportunity offered, she embarked with her two companions, one of whom had never forsaken her, in a fishing-boat, and crossed in a few hours that main on whose expanse they had suffered such prolonged distress. Tomas had gone off the moment they landed to his parents on the beach.

" But," said old Maddis, who had ventured to steal up-stairs, and stood wiping his eyes at the door, " I thought I 'd see her safe with her *pailo;* she has sorrowed enough for that rosy cheek; and Jewess though she be, nobody better deserves to become a Christian. I 'm not sure she is not one already."

We cannot quite vouch for the truth of good Maddis's surmise, but this we can assert, that Rose never quitted her benefactress, and that the little Matvei was baptized a fortnight afterwards at the village church.

THE END

London · Printed by WILLIAM CLOWES and SONS, Stamford Street.

**DO NOT REMOVE
SLIP FROM POCKET**

Check Out More Titles From HardPress Classics Series In this collection we are offering thousands of classic and hard to find books. This series spans a vast array of subjects – so you are bound to find something of interest to enjoy reading and learning about.

Subjects:
Architecture
Art
Biography & Autobiography
Body, Mind &Spirit
Children & Young Adult
Dramas
Education
Fiction
History
Language Arts & Disciplines
Law
Literary Collections
Music
Poetry
Psychology
Science
…and many more.

Visit us at www.hardpress.net

SD - #0026 - 160622 - C0 - 229/152/11 - PB - 9780461085334 - Gloss Lamination